CREATING PRODUCTS AND BUSINESSES THAT MARKET THEMSELVES

ALEX BOGUSKY & JOHN WINSOR

A B2 Book

AGATE

CHICAGO

Illustrations by Conor McCann
Layout by Marco Merced and Cathy Dickinson

Copyright © 2009 Crispin Porter + Bogusky LLC
All rights reserved. No part of this book may be reproduced or
transmitted in any form or by any means, electronic or mechanical,
including photocopying, recording, or by any information storage
and retrieval system, without express written permission from the
publisher.
Printed in Canada.

Trade paperback edition
ISBN-13: 978-1-932841-57-2, ISBN-10: 1-932841-57-1

The Library of Congress has cataloged the hardcover edition of this
book as follows:
Library of Congress Cataloging-in-Publication Data

Bogusky, A. M. (Alex M.)
Baked in : creating products and businesses that market themselves
/ Alex Bogusky and John Winsor.
    p. cm.
Summary: "Advertising leaders Bogusky and Winsor discuss
the latest trends in product innovation as the key to cutting-edge
marketing"--Provided by publisher.
ISBN-13: 978-1-932841-46-6 (hbk. : alk. paper)
ISBN-10: 1-932841-46-6 (hbk. : alk. paper)
1. New products. 2. Advertising--New products. 3. Marketing. I.
Winsor, John, 1959- II. Title.

 HF5415.153.B64 2009
 658.5'75--dc22
                           2009012079
10 11 12 13   10 9 8 7 6 5 4 3 2 1

B2 Books is an imprint of Agate Publishing. Agate books
are available in bulk at discount prices. For more information,
go to agatepublishing.com.

TABLE OF → CONTENTS

"More than a book, this is a workbook. If you're serious about overhauling the way your organization does marketing, here's a great place to start."

-Seth Godin, Author, Meatball Sundae

"If you want to understand the future of marketing, advertising and product design, start here. *Baked In* provides essential insights from two of the hottest minds in marketing today."

-Chris Anderson, Author, Free *and* The Long Tail

"Everything's changing. The Old Order is no more. Welcome to The Participation Economy. Welcome to the unreasonable power of Creativity. Welcome to *Baked In.*"

-Kevin Roberts, CEO, Saatchi & Saatchi Worldwide, Author, Lovemarks

"This book hit me like all great ideas hit me: it's profound, but also so simple I wonder why someone hasn't already expressed the idea. Alex and John—two ad guys—make the case that marketing and advertising as we have known it is obsolete."

-Brian Dunn, CEO, Best Buy

"Alex Bogusky and John Winsor are calling for a new holy alliance in the crusade to make business more innovative and the world a more interesting place. *Baked In* challenges us to break down the silos between design and marketing and invite everybody in. It gives us a peek into a future where as consumers, designers and marketers we all get our hands dirty in the messy, creative process of making new products and markets."

-*Tim Brown, CEO, IDEO*

"As cogent and inspiring a plan for the future of marketing and advertising as you could hope for—from two of the leading practitioners of the age. Read it now, before everyone else has."

-*Mark Earls, Author,* Herd *and* Welcome to the Creative Age

"With *Baked In*, Alex Bogusky and John Winsor recast the way people will think about the integration of marketing and product design. This is a provocative and compelling message, and vision for the future."

-*Matt Jacobson, Head of Market Development, Facebook*

ACKNOWLEDGEMENTS

It certainly takes a village to write a book. We must start with a huge thanks to Ana Bogusky and Bridget Winsor. Their patience was certainly stretched thin, but they tried to hide it as we worked from home to find the peace and quiet that doesn't exist at the office. And for good reason: it is an advertising agency, after all. Chaos is as important there as paper clips are in most offices. We'd also like to thank Ana and Bridget for their guidance on the contents (and spelling and grammar) in the book. Thanks to the many friends on Twitter, on Facebook, and throughout the blogosphere who contributed ideas about companies that should be included in the story of *Baked In*. Co-creation is fun, and it works. Thanks to Erin Larsen for blocking out time on our schedules to allow us to go hide and write and for all of her help in organizing the multiple piles of disconnected thoughts into a single pile of what we hope are interconnected thoughts. Finally, we owe a huge debt of gratitude to all the companies we have had the pleasure to research and get to know a bit better through this process. They are not just leading the way in innovation, but we've come to see them as leading the way to what we believe will ultimately be a new, more aware, and completely sustainable form of free enterprise.

PART ONE:

PREHEAT YOUR MIND

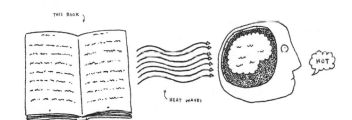

We all have lots of preconceived notions about the world of products and marketing. So let's begin by preheating your mind before we get to the baking.

You enter a big room that's filled with machines. Against one wall is a machine that looks like a big microwave oven. As you peer into the machine's window, you're a bit disappointed to find a pair of sunglasses that appear to have been cut in half horizontally. The color, though, is just what you had hoped for. The machine is hard at work, so you decide to go get a cup of coffee. By the time you come back, the glasses are carefully formed. You then try them on to check the prescription. Perfect. And the coolest part of all is that you're not on the starship *Enterprise*. You're at Kinko's (now FedEx Office).

Consider the 3D printer. When the term was first used in print, it was hard to imagine such a thing could exist. To be able to "print out" an object in three dimensions has been the stuff of science fiction for a long time. But today, such devices exist. Many of us have still never seen one, but we can say with full confidence that they exist because at Crispin Porter + Bogusky (CP+B), we actually own one. It probably wouldn't surprise you to learn that to own this modern marvel required an investment in excess of a million dollars. But what might surprise you is that is, in fact, a lie: It cost a little under $20,000.

Consider the power in that. In the past, creating prototypes was a very time-consuming and laborious process that has now been fundamentally boiled down to pressing a print button. This is just one aspect of the technology and processes that are compressing the production time frame of products from years to months—and in some cases, even weeks. We're not talking about cutting-edge technology here, either. The software we use to design and make 3D models of the products that then get sent to this magical printer is the very same software that is being taught to the junior high students who go to school down the street. It's a new world. The new shop class doesn't teach you how to repair a car. It teaches you the tools that allow you to design and manufacture your own line of vehicles.

The democratization of the printed word until recently was referred to as the desktop publishing revolution. Today, we can hardly remember a time when any individual couldn't create and print out whatever was on his or her mind. And the revolution went way beyond where even the revolutionaries expected it to go—because who needs paper? Blogging made the idea of publishing on paper arcane.

Well, what the computer did in two dimensions, it's now doing in three, and the democratization of product design has begun. The 3D printer will continue to improve. Today, most 3D printers create plastic prototypes, but that is already changing as newer models have the capability to print in multiple materials. Circuit boards are already created in a process that is fundamentally printing. And these circuit boards make up the inner workings of most consumer electronics. How long will it be before fully working prototypes can be printed? Probably not very long. And once we're capable of printing fully working products, why even bother to manufacture in traditional terms? Why not just print more? Or why not just sell the idea and the plans for a product instead of the product itself? Customers can make their changes and print it out themselves.

Marketing people like to say that product is more than a physical object. As in a cup of coffee is more than a cup of coffee. A pair of sunglasses is more than a pair of sunglasses. A car is more than a car. There's a story that the car represents. A promise. And that's what we're really selling. That's what the brand is made of.

Sometimes this story is true, and sometimes, unfortunately, it's not. Sometimes a car really is just a car. So the process of marketing is to uncover, coax out, and tell a story that is buried inside the product. Most of the time a story can be found, but too often the story is only tenuously connected to the product, and in some cases the story is just wishful thinking on the part of all the marketers around the table. Perhaps the product was created without a clear narrative and audience in mind or is just another me-too product with nothing new to offer. What happens next is too often the sad state of affairs that passes for marketing. A battery of focus groups, ethnographies, brain scans, and more are arranged to go forth and uncover what the consumer wishes the product really was. Then the marketing budget is spent telling lies about the product.

This book is about flipping that process.

In today's world—in the same amount of time it takes to create an advertising campaign—it's now possible to take all that consumer insight and actually *bake it right into a new product*. A product designed with a mission. A product with a story to tell. A product with the ability to sell itself.

Can your organization create a product like this?

THE SEEDS OF A NEW DESIGN

Today there are some amazing examples of companies and products in which marketing and product design are being connected, and in the future there will be many more examples. But some of our favorite examples of this are actually a couple hundred years old; yet they still demonstrate the power unleashed when product and marketing spring from the same well of inspiration, fueled by the same stories and beliefs.

The Shakers, also known as the United Society

of Believers in Christ's Second Appearing, started in 1747, in Manchester, England, as an offshoot of the Quaker faith. Both groups believed that everybody could find God within him- or herself, rather than through the clergy or through church-based rituals, and that their lives should be dedicated to glorifying God through their work.

In 1774, one of the group's leaders, Mother Ann Lee, brought nine of her followers to the United States. Over the next century, the Shakers grew to 19 communities and 6,000 members. A cornerstone of the Shaker religion was the belief that work was an act of prayer. Everything from crafting a chair to planting a seed to cleaning a home should be done with the same diligence a follower would bring to honoring God. Mother Ann Lee herself once wrote, "Do all of your work as though you had a thousand years to live, and as you would if you knew you must die tomorrow."

Out of this philosophy of combining hard work with the pursuit of perfection, the Shakers created a unique style of architecture, furniture, and handcrafts that include their now legendary boxes and brooms. Their designs were known for their use of simple materials and construction that combined elegance and practicality. This constituted a strong core "narrative" behind the products they created.

Out of this Shaker narrative came many product

innovations. The Shakers invented the rotary harrow, the circular saw, the clothespin, the flat broom, and the wheel-driven washing machine, among other things. They were also the country's largest producer of medicinal herbs. But it was the selling of their famous garden seeds that would lead to their accidental discovery of branding and marketing.

Somewhere around 1790, the Shakers started selling their seeds to outsiders to earn money for their communities. Their garden seeds were known for their ability to produce high yields of vegetables. At first, it was easy to sell the seeds, when they were dealing solely with stores in towns close to Shaker communities. These folks were well aware of the Shaker story and their reputation as seed producers.

But as the Shakers' seeds started to travel farther from their communities, fewer people knew the Shaker story. In an effort to sell their seeds in new places, the Shakers started to take their seeds out of generic bins and box them in beautifully designed pine boxes that could be used as packages and counter displays. They even added hand-painted logos on the outside of the boxes. And they branded their seeds, labeling them as "Shaker Seeds." It's worth noting here that the term "Shaker" was originally pejorative, derived from the term "Shaking Quakers," which mocked their rituals of singing, shouting, and shaking while worshipping. Much as Budweiser would do with its brand by embracing the name "Bud" in the late twentieth century, the Shakers didn't shy away from the name their customers called them. The seeds and the packaging could be used to go out into the world and tell the Shaker story that the Shakers themselves couldn't be there to tell. After a few years, the Shakers even started using individual paper-envelope packages for their seeds—the same packages that are common for seeds today. So not only did the Shakers' product itself tell an important story, but they had also created the packaging innovations that helped the seeds sell themselves. (Ironically, this innovation would be one of the last in the seed-selling business. It's probably time for another.)

To some, it may seem surprising that a culture so focused on religious faith was able to be so good at both marketing and product design. Yet neither would have been possible without the powerful narrative that guided everything the Shakers did. The distance that their relationship with God created between themselves and their customers was also important here. The Shakers had no choice; the *only* way they could succeed was to bake their marketing right into the product.

Today, marketing and product design remain largely disconnected ideas. As shaped by the realities of the Industrial Revolution, companies have long developed structures that have built walls between these two important parts of their businesses. The functional silos that exist now in many companies are a legacy from a time when product platform timelines were measured in years, or even decades. There wasn't any real reason for marketing and product design to be integrated. In fact, a heads-up meeting was all about getting the cooperation that either party required. The needs of consumers, and of companies, have obviously changed, but these legacy structures still stand in many companies. And they stand in the way.

This is made apparent by looking at how different functions are involved in the internal organizational structure at most companies today. Advertising and marketing are usually viewed as strategic efforts made with the involvement of chief executive officers (CEOs) and chief marketing officers (CMOs). Yet many companies' product decisions are made at a much lower level, usually among product managers. The day-to-day iteration of a product isn't necessarily seen as having a lot of strategic or marketing implications. This structure has created a situation where marketing tells one story about the company, usually connected to corporate strategy at the senior level, while the products tell several stories, depending on a product manager's vision of his or her own strategy. This problem is compounded by the fact that product people either don't see or aren't rewarded for understanding the role of the company's brand in the form a product takes.

WHAT'S STANDING IN THE WAY?

Corporate structures have gotten in the way of the momentum creativity can generate. The product design team works for months doing research and creating designs. Sometimes this design has a brand narrative, but more often than not, the story—if it ever existed—is lost in the design process, falling victim to bad focus groups, or perhaps an egocentric designer with an overly personal agenda. If by some miracle a product does make it through this random process with a perceptible story intact, and the team then hands it off to the marketing department, the design narrative is almost invariably discarded in order for the marketing team to start all over again. To make matters worse, advertising agencies often create yet another narrative for the product. When the marketing finally appears, there are four possible outcomes:

1. The product has no story, and neither does the marketing.
2. The product has no story, but the marketing makes one up anyway.
3. The product has a story, but the marketing tells a different one.
4. The product has a story, and the marketing makes it sing.

There is only one acceptable outcome here. So where do we start? How do we create a process that makes this the rule instead of the exception?

For many companies, it's time to break down these internal silos and realize that collaboration is at the heart of this new marketing/innovation paradigm. While collaboration with customers is key, the ability to collaborate internally is even more important. Businesses and their brands are built through great, innovative products. Branding and marketing must be reconnected to the products themselves. The goal of a new design process should be to elevate both marketing and product design together at the strategic level, fueled by the same powerful narrative. So brilliant designers and marketers must work together to create products that are consistent in form and story.

RETHINK. RESTRUCTURE. RECOMMIT.

The world today has forced us to accept change as an integral part of business. It is either innovate or die. It may be surprising to those of us who fear change, but innovation is actually part of our human DNA. Here is how science puts it, in the words of Geoffrey A. Moore in his book *Dealing with Darwin: How Great Companies Innovate at Every Phase of Their Evolution*: "Evolution requires us to continually refresh our competitive advantage. To innovate forever is not an aspiration; it is a design specification. It is not a strategy; it is a requirement."

Today, brands exist in a rapidly changing marketplace. In the blink of an eye, brands can go from being winners to losers. They face new pressures exerted by digital technologies, globalization, cultural diversity, economic recalibration, and the sheer volume and variety of available products and brands. These pressures are forcing companies to rethink everything from advertising to product design and, if they're smart enough, even the basic structures of their businesses.

Likewise, the new ways in which consumers demand to get involved with products, from producing them themselves to co-creating them with a company, change our concept of manufacturing. Even the way consumers communicate among themselves and the companies they do business with have blurred the lines between producer, consumer, retailer, and advertiser. These changes demand that every company engage with its customers in new ways.

Digital tools have empowered everyone with the ability to effect change through his or her own creativity. Many traditional barriers to entry have collapsed. Want to have a voice? Start a blog. Want to make a product? Start a company. Likewise, new design tools accelerate production times for everything. Cool idea? Design it on a laptop. E-mail it to a factory anywhere in the world, and in a matter of days, the designer can have a product in consumers' hands. This is already old news, as the advances in the 3D printers we talked about earlier will, sooner than most of us may think, make it possible to design and share ideas digitally, allowing consumers to render products at places like FedEx Office. For example: Design a shoe. Your customers customize it at home. After an hour or so, they drop by their local product printer, produce them, lace them up and they're ready to rock and roll. Not long after that, we'll be "printing" some of the smaller, simpler products at home. Eventually, we'll only go to FedEx Office to print out the big stuff. Like cars.

A BRIEF HISTORY OF BRANDING

To create some context for what's before us, we need to take a step back to understand what created the current brand/product paradigm. Brands became important during the Industrial Revolution to describe a whole new idea: mass-produced goods. The brand became a way consumers could identify the consistency some of these goods offered. Pillsbury flour and Morton salt offered far more reliable quality than no-name goods. The brand had the job of quickly identifying a product and telling a story consistent with the product. Early industrialization techniques meant that the product would differ very little from year to year, and it would even differ very little from its competitors. It became marketing's job to inject news and excitement into what was essentially a consistent, unchanging product. This culminated in the late part of the twentieth century, when pretty much all products were described as "parity products," all the same, all on a par with one another.

This situation created an advertising and marketing bonanza. If everything was the same, then only the spin could make them feel different to consumers. In this situation, there was really no reason for production and marketing to speak to each other. The product development progress was so slow, the marketing people could read about their own innovation in the newspaper.

That was then. The new age has come upon us so fast that we didn't have time to change how we think, or how we're structured. Consumers—and a select group of innovative companies—have sailed into this new world, while most corporations sit on the shore, watching the sea and still believing the world is flat.

WELCOME TO BRANDING 2001. YOU'RE LATE.

Today, companies are being built without advertising in a way that would have been impossible not long ago. Some of the greatest of today's brands go to market with their products without much advertising support at all. How can this be?

Until recently, Starbucks was a great example. For a long time, its coffee and shops—its products—were its sole marketing tools. Not only did Starbucks do it without advertising, but it is very likely the company would have failed to grow as quickly as it did if the company had used advertising.

Wait. Did we just say advertising would have hurt Starbucks' ability to grow? Yes. Because word of mouth can actually be shut off by using traditional advertising. Starbucks was able to use simple cardboard signs in its locations to introduce new products. Now, a company like McDonald's couldn't do that because such companies use television for that purpose, and we all know it. If you see a sign for a new product at McDonald's and you think your friends might like it, you would never bother to tell them about it because your assumption is that they will learn about it on TV. (Unfortunately for McDonald's, though, that's an unrealistic assumption when today's top-rated prime-time show reaches fewer than 2 percent of the U.S. population.)

Starbucks could use cardboard signs to introduce new products in its stores because we all knew Starbucks didn't advertise. Knowing about the latest Frappuccino drink was a little piece of cultural currency you could spend the next time you saw one of your coffee-loving friends. The advertising was not just baked into the Frappuccino along with its sweet goodness, addictive caffeine, and beautiful name, but into the fact that *Starbucks allowed you to be part of telling its story.* And Starbucks did it as much by what it didn't do as what it did.

Starbucks didn't advertise—at least not in the conventional way most of us think of advertising.

The vacuum of communication that traditional advertising leaves in its absence can be filled by consumers—consumers anxious to take part in helping tell the story of products and companies they love.

There are lots of examples, including Patagonia, Jones Soda, and Zara. Zara, a global clothing retailer, has never run an advertising campaign; yet it launches 10,000 new designs each year in its more than 1,000 shops worldwide. The company innovated by dramatically reducing the time from inspiration to in-store product, allowing it to stay months ahead of its competitors. And that is a story worth telling.

Today, the old concept of how a brand works must be called into question. Exactly what a brand can *be* has changed radically in just the last few years, but what brands will *become* is changing right now. Will "brand" even remain a concept worth thinking about, or will it be replaced by something more evolved? Will being a great brand be a kind of consolation prize? It seems like that is already happening. It seems like every day there is the business failure of another "great brand"; so just how important can a "great brand" be? It's certainly not enough anymore.

With the collapse of the old advertising and marketing models, it's critical that companies wake up to the fact that the product itself is the most powerful brand-building and business tool they have. All the advertising agencies and branding experts that seduced those companies into thinking marketing was the best way to connect with consumers need to wake up, too. The old structures and old ways of thinking mean companies continue to underestimate consumers' ability to recognize and respond to innovation very rapidly. Even with innumerable examples all around us, we cling to a process of slow product evolution. Today, the ability to innovate is not only the best marketing tool but also the best way to grow revenues and profits.

One of the main reasons why this is true today turns out to be very simple. Most products are marketed to reach an old market, so they can hope to steal a point or so of market share. Innovative product design, however, has the ability to create an entirely new market. For example, Apple could have entered the MP3 player market. Instead, it invented both the iPod and iTunes, and created a new way to buy and share music. Now Apple has 75 percent of the player market and about 85 percent of online music sales. You can't "advertise" your way to that kind of growth—you have to innovate and create something new.

Likewise, companies that are built by using mass marketing tend to develop their products similarly. They round the edges, smooth out the differentiating features, and try to make products that work for the masses. They use focus groups to make sure products are "acceptable." These products certainly don't offend anyone, but acceptable is always the most risky strategy, because acceptable is failing at an astounding rate in today's marketing environment. And what's even scarier is that we don't seem able to recognize all these failures because we don't notice these failing products to begin with. So when they go away, it's as if nothing happened, no Harvard case histories, no headlines, and no news stories. It would be like a headline from *The Onion:* "Product that nobody noticed discontinued. Reporter too bored to ask any questions."

On the other hand, the stuff we notice is the stuff we tend to buy. This has proven to be a hard lesson for many companies to learn. We hate to pick on the American auto industry at times like these. In fact, there seemed to be a time after the disastrous launch of the Pontiac Aztek when it looked like GM had figured things out. Do you remember that car? It was hailed as a "game changer," but it didn't change the game in the way Pontiac had imagined. It was too obvious a product of consumer focus groups, designed as though to please everyone on the planet at the same time. The Aztek was considered by many to be the ugliest car ever made.

After the Aztek debacle, it looked like the power to design products had been put back in the hands of Detroit's designers and innovators. The next few years saw a new Cadillac emerge, as well as a fleet of good-looking cars from Chrysler, including the 300.

It looked like even Ford was getting it. But this was short lived. As organizations, the Big Three just didn't know how to innovate anymore. It was as though it had been bred out of their corporate DNA. So they missed the chance to have fuel-efficient cars when the public wanted them. At the same time, many of the tools they had relied on so heavily, like traditional advertising, had lost their power, and they didn't have any news any of us wanted to spread among our friends.

Today, customers are more and more demanding. They want products that are perfectly tailored to satisfy their needs. They want to have a say in their creation. And whether you like it or not, with technology platforms like YouTube and Twitter, they will also communicate to the world how and why they love or hate your product, your brand, and your company. If you don't have what they want, they'll either get it from a competitor somewhere else in the world or perhaps build it themselves.

That means your customers demand to be involved with your company. They want to participate in building a brand they will become loyal to, generating a conversation around new ideas, and manufacturing products that will speak to their needs. These customers back and appreciate the brands they love.

We understand we might sound a little confusing or contradictory here. Yes, we just said that overly focus-grouped products are guilty of creating uninspired, me-too goods that have put whole industries at peril. Now we're saying companies should get in bed with these same meddling, opinionated consumers. This is a bit of a contradiction; but as with most things in life, it's not *what* you do, it's *how* you do it.

In our experience, focus groups have a really odd dynamic generated by people known among researchers as the "Alpha Asshole." This is the person who is most comfortable being opinionated among a group of strangers. Such people tend to create a skewed result in these settings, because the more polite folks in the group just go along. What kind of sane person wants to get into an unpleasant difference of opinion with some loudmouth just because they're being paid 50 bucks for their opinion? Unfortunately, sometimes this means companies are left with only the non-sane opinion among an entire focus group. Another issue with focus groups is that consumers tend to use comparisons to provide their expertise, and if there is nothing to compare an idea to they will often just reject it. After all, you are paying them 50 bucks for their opinion. So even if it's well outside their area of expertise, they feel they have to say *something*. This can be a big problem if you are trying to uncover reactions to true innovation.

A couple of different strategies work well in countering these focus group issues. One is to speak with consumers organized among groups of friends. This prevents the Alpha Asshole from being too dominant, because even the more polite members of this kind of group will call BS on true BS. The other strategy is to come to a group with ideas and actually invite participants into the creative process—not with a blank sheet of paper, but with lots of stimulus to spur their thinking. Finally, always be aware that truly innovative ideas almost always generate at least some debate, if not outright fear. If something is universally loved, it might be quite nice, but it's likely been done before. In general, it turns out people tend to work best when you treat them like well, people, not test subjects. Go figure.

Back in the real world, and armed with their new interactive tools, today's new consumers research products, brands, and corporate cultures; share their buying experiences and rate them; create a positive or negative halo around a brand; and generally participate in shaping the public perceptions of a brand. The customer, more than ever, is in control. The only thing consumers really trust is true peer-to-peer input: personal stories of products they love. Many expect even more: they seek brands and products that have relevant (to them) social values and rich symbolic meaning embedded in them. If you can be more human, and thus more willing to have a conversation with these consumers, they will let you into their communities, and you will reap the benefits that come with that sort of access.

The walls that exist between the departments in an antiquated business structure and the walls that exist between consumers and companies, have a couple of important things in common. First, they're both bad for business. And second, they both have to come down before your organization can harness the power of building innovation and marketing products that can market themselves.

SAY GOODBYE TO THE EIGHTIES

It's been over for a long time—the bad hair, the bad music, the parity products, and the prime-time advertising. Brands will be built on the basis of a new relationship among products, their consumers, and the surrounding culture.

The old way was: Create safe, ordinary products and combine them with mass marketing. One thing you'll notice about the chart on the next page is that the farther you get from the product, the more expensive the communications become. What you might not recognize is that the power of those brand interactions decrease as you get farther from the center, too.

The new way is: Create truly innovative products and build the marketing right into them. Layer after layer of this interaction are all designed to carry

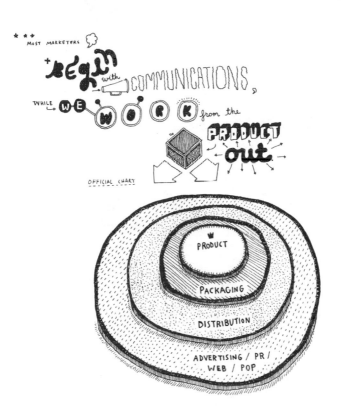

MOST MARKETERS BEGIN with COMMUNICATIONS, WHILE WE WORK from the PRODUCT out

OFFICIAL CHART

PRODUCT

PACKAGING

DISTRIBUTION

ADVERTISING / PR / WEB / POP

the same narrative: the product, the packaging, the environment, the distribution, the web, the advertising. All of it says the same thing. If it's done well enough, there isn't much need for media advertising by the time you get to the outer layer.

Creativity has become the ultimate business weapon. The same creativity that's been used to change culture through advertising can also be applied to distribution, packaging, and even—you guessed it—the product itself. Applying creativity to every facet of a business makes it possible to change fortunes almost overnight.

BECAUSE THE MOST POWERFUL BRAND EXPERIENCES & CONNECTIONS BEGIN WITH THE PRODUCT

NEW — EST. XXXX —

OFFICIAL CHART

PRODUCT

PACKAGING

DIGITAL

DISTRIBUTION

ADVERTISING

BAKE IN THE MARKETING FROM THE START

Getting people together to co-create the narrative for a product and its marketing—in a collaborative way that creates a singular voice for a brand—can generate unstoppable momentum. And it is happening every day. But it's not always easy. To be successful in the new world, product design and innovation must move way up the corporate ladder to join marketing at the company's strategic center.

Today, the product can and should be the center of the marketing conversation. The product will be your most powerful marketing tool. So if you're a CEO, where should your attention be going? If you're a CMO, where should your attention be going? But that's not at all what is happening. That's why in many bigger companies, the product tells one story and the marketing tells another, different story. GM's Hummer product design shouts power and overindulgence. Yet the advertising tries to tell a story of a Zen-like experience and exploration. What's the end goal in all of this? The marketing is actually being put to use to try to correct issues the product creates. And it does so quite brilliantly. But what a waste of money to say one thing with the industrial design and the actual product creation, and find through consumer research that you have to try to take it back with the marketing. Yikes.

WE INTERRUPT THIS BOOK FOR A MESSAGE ABOUT THE ECONOMY

As of right now, the economy is experiencing a downturn of truly historic proportions. And there is a good chance that this economic context has you more concerned with cost cutting than product innovation. It must surely seem counterintuitive (to many, at least) to be more innovative when the economy struggles, so let us offer some thoughts on the subject.

First, if one were to look at a list of the 2008 *Inc.* 500 companies, you would notice that more than half of them had one thing in common. They all started in the few months following 9/11. The people who started those companies decided to make an opportunity of the uncertainty created by the events of that day. Sometimes, it's just natural for creative people to forget about the uncertainty and focus on innovation, but their success points to market conditions in times of flux that favor innovative ideas.

When the macroenvironment changes radically, as it is doing today, it's easy to be gripped with fear and focus on efficiency. But when the old ideas are failing, customers are more open to innovative thinking. *Now* is the time when bold innovations will find their greatest audience. The most damaging thing any of us can do is get locked up by fear and insecurity. If you pull in your horns waiting for things to get better, they certainly will—but not necessarily for you. Business is going to get better, but it will improve most for those who put fear out of their mind and move forward aggressively.

Disruptive times always create opportunities for companies. In the 1970s, both Microsoft and Apple were founded in the middle of an economically turbulent time. Likewise, in the middle of a recession, Palm shifted from being a software company to a hardware company, and invented a whole new industry as a result. The biggest problems at times like these are new problems, and only innovative thinking will solve a new problem. As Einstein said, "No problem can be solved from the same level of consciousness that created it."

You will find nothing in this book about investing in a new, bigger "process." On the contrary: This book is about breaking down barriers and creating new means for innovation that use intelligence from more quarters of an organization in a flatter, more streamlined, nimbler way, to bring smarter ideas to market faster. You'll find that *Baked In* and rightsizing have a lot in common. Bloated organizations will never be places of great innovation. Everyone will be reenvisioning their organizations during this downturn; why not transform your business into a lean product/marketing juggernaut?

THE SINGLE MOST POWERFUL MARKETING TOOL

By now you are beginning to realize that we don't think the most powerful tool is a Super Bowl ad. It's not any kind television advertising at all. And it isn't magazines or newspapers or radio or even the Web (though we have to disclaim the Web here, because sometimes, the Web can actually *be* the product).

Nope. In all our years of doing all of the above, we've found (at times to our dismay) that the *product* is always the most powerful brand-building marketing and sales tool. The ability to innovate is not only the best marketing tool, but it's also the best way to grow revenue and profits. It provides the most direct connection to the consumer.

Great product design creates whole new markets. And while great products can create an instant brand, they can also be created from existing brands that either have uncovered or can uncover a powerful and consistent story that runs through everything about the product. In this way, instead of marketing and advertising falling to the back end of the process, it is baked in right up front.

Our baked-in approach to marketing and product design starts with the same cultural and consumer research and strategy that companies' product groups and marketing groups have long been doing separately and essentially combines them into one process.

Marketing has a seat at the table with product. Product has a seat at the table with marketing. And the deliverable isn't product or marketing. The deliverable is both. This process yields a strategy and a narrative that can fuel not only the product alone but also the marketing, distribution, and *everything else* the brand is trying to do with the product.

THE NEW APPROACH

allocate RESOURCES to THE PRODUCT → BAKING THE MARKETING INTO IT – FOR A STRONGER CONSUMER/BRAND CONNECTION.

CULTURAL RESEARCH

CONSUMER RESEARCH

PRODUCT THAT MARKETS ITSELF

WEAPONIZED CREATIVITY

The main goal of *Baked In* is to show that creativity is the ultimate business weapon. It's not too hard to convince people of this idea. They've seen it in other organizations. What's harder to convince people of is that they can take a *systematic* approach to brilliant ideas.

Creativity is like anthrax. It's extremely potent, but it's hard to distribute. So to "weaponize" anthrax is to figure out a way to distribute it quickly and widely. (This is an annoying analogy for a couple of peaceful guys such as ourselves, but you get the point.) We want to weaponize creativity and innovation in your organization. To the detriment of anybody who didn't read this book.

The rest of this book is a set of rules for how to develop a better narrative foundation for both better marketing and better products. It will help you bake your marketing right into your products as you design them. If you haven't already taken the leap, we'll help you make the transition to the new paradigm, where a brand's products and marketing not only tell the same story but also have a deep connection to culture and the flexibility to be extraordinary.

The best first step with anything new is always to jump right in. And you have. You bought this book, and so you're ready to open your mind and experience new things. But this book isn't what you thought it was. It seemed stable enough when you bought it. It has a nice sturdy cover and is filled with letters that are permanently inked on the page. Yet it's already changing and morphing into a better version of what it needs to be for its readers. The minute the first copy was sold, this book started the process of making itself better. To fully experience this book, you'll need to be on Twitter. You probably already are, but if you're a CEO or something, you might not be, so go ahead and take five minutes to do it, or ask somebody to do it for you. We'll wait.

Well done. Now where were we?

It seems the best way to understand the new creativity and baked-in marketing is to experience it. So to that end, we've included both a feedback mechanism and a way to experience the *Baked In* discussion in real time.

Throughout the book you will see our Twitter address, @bakedin. You can find the discussion there or just type in @bakedin when you post a comment and then anybody can search out your post. We'll also include a Twitter hash mark after each recipe. They look like this: #example. These hash marks can narrow the search to just that chapter.

We'll be collecting, scanning, and replying to the comments to create a better next edition; but more important for you readers, this book can become so much more for you than just what you're holding in your hands. It can be an interactive experience that will get your mind racing as you play and experiment and critique while you're reading.

PART TWO:

28 RULES FOR BAKING IN

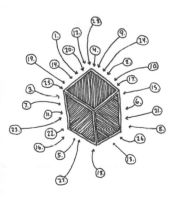

CULTURE TRUMPS INFLUENCERS

There's a theory in marketing that if you talk to the right people about a product, then they will talk to more right people, and pretty soon you will reach a "tipping point," à la Malcolm Gladwell's book of the same name. Well, about a year ago, Duncan Watts blew that theory out of the water.

Duncan Watts is a researcher at Columbia who currently works at Yahoo! as a researcher in residence. With access to the Yahoo! network of members, Watts has repeated Stanley Milgram's famous experiment that proved his theory of six degrees of separation. In the original 1967 experiment, Milgram gave 300 people in Nebraska and Kansas envelopes addressed to a stockbroker in Boston. The only rule was that they had to send it to someone they knew. The envelopes found their way to the stockbroker in an amazing average of 5.5 stops along the way.

When Watts tried to duplicate these experiments digitally, he was also able to examine how trends start and what role influencers play in trends. Much to our delight (we've always been fans of cultural pressures as motivators), Watts found that influencers are less influential than the tipping point model would have us believe. Watts argues that news travels as readily through ordinary people as influential ones. We are just as likely to hear something from a friend as we are from a networking maven. This means our world is not "hub and spoke," like the flight-network model built by the airlines (with the influencers or mavens as the hubs). Instead, interpersonal networks are more democratic.

As Watts has said, "If society is ready to embrace a trend, almost anyone can start [one]. If it isn't, then almost no one can." According to Watts, trends start and culture changes much more randomly than we suspected. We believe that, at its core, culture always *wants* to change—especially pop culture. In fact, change is its whole job. Cultural change is always imminent, waiting for random events, either large or small, that will push it over the edge. In the end, cultural change is the product of an alchemy of events and individual influence. As the cultural conditions change, the change is expressed in particular events; influencers become early detectors of this change and communicate it to the rest of the community.

A great example of this alchemy is And1's (one of CP+B's former clients) influence on the world of basketball. In the late 1990s, And1 was trying to break into the basketball shoe business. This was proving to be difficult, as the big competitor was probably the greatest marketing company of all time: Nike, which had a great product and most of the greatest pro athletes locked up as endorsers, too. And1 had risen by selling playground-inspired apparel. The playground basketball game was very different from the world of the NBA. It was grittier, but played with a sense of style and artistic expression that sometimes meant the score was secondary to the moves. And these playground moves were moves most of us consumers had never seen—half athletic prowess and half magic. Not coincidentally, one of the best street ballers of the time went by the nickname of Half Man, Half Amazing. But these athletes and this kind of basketball were considered inferior to the NBA style. Their stories were usually stories of talent gone tragically unfulfilled.

It was our opinion that this could all change. It could be a perfect marriage. And1 couldn't afford NBA players, so we thought, *let's sign and promote playground players*. Let's treat them with the respect they deserve. People were skeptical. The prevailing sentiment was that this game and these players were irrelevant. An And1 partner put the sentiment clearly when presented with the idea: "No kid is going to buy a pair of shoes because some playground player is wearing them."

"They will if we make them famous," we said.

Soon we were working on creating the first And1 mix tape. A VHS tape of the most outrageous playground ball we could capture from coast to coast set to just-released hip-hop. Performers from the hip-hop community were giving us music to drop onto the tapes because we were showing love to something they loved: playground ball and the players. And at the beginning, you could only get the tapes with a purchase of select And1 shoes. The tape that was being sold with the shoe was actually making the shoe and the company famous. The commercial was part of the purchase.

Over the years, we produced a lot of tapes, as did Nike and Adidas and others. Playground players were eventually signed to contracts by all the same companies. In the end, *Sports Illustrated* ran an article bemoaning the fact that nobody wanted to use NBA players to promote shoes anymore. The culture had flipped. But it would be wrong to say And1 flipped the culture. No. The conditions were right and And1 became the catalyst in the alchemy of culture that kicked off the chain reaction. Oh, and its business went from 50 million to 300 million along the way.

RECIPE

Make a list of the cultural trends that influence your consumers' behavior. Take your time; all of the items on this list will not be immediately apparent. Stay with it, and you will gradually observe more and more. Be a good observer. Remove yourself from your own cultural perspective. Look for the absurdities, the incongruities, the things that don't necessarily make sense. You will begin to laugh as you start to see the culture from the outside. (Laughing is a good sign.)

Find out what's really beneath the existing trend. Is the truth under the truth? Use the And1 example: Was it that NBA stars sold sneakers because they were in the NBA, or because they were famous ball players? If it is the latter, then any famous basketball player can sell shoes. So let's make somebody new famous. Let's create the fame to create the sales.

In your business, what is the accepted cultural convention? If you get the right fix on this, you can flip it on its head and make it your own.

Twitter @Bakedin #Convention

BROADEN YOUR DEFINITION OF DESIGN

Our friend Bruce Mau is a designer who is probably most well known for an exhibit he put together called Massive Change. And Massive Change, as Bruce sees it, is not so much about the world of design as it is about the design of the world. He looks at product design as the entire system of your business: how you source your materials, how you manufacture, how you distribute and sell, and what happens to your products after the consumer is done with them.

A perfectly designed system would have no waste, but most products are far from achieving this virtuous cycle. In fact, many of the brands we know and love are filling landfills with their products and their logos (a PR disaster that has yet to come home to roost—

but it's coming).

When you look at design in this broader context, you gain a broader range of things to consider when it comes to baking in your marketing. You also realize that this means many more of us are now "designers" than we realized.

If you entered the plastic fork business, we would think your chances for runaway success would be pretty limited in this very mature category. But Eco-Products saw its business grow 500 percent in 2008, and it's projecting the same for 2009. Eco-Products is a company that developed biodegradable, disposable utensils. These knives, forks, and spoons are made primarily from vegetable starch. They can be composted and will biodegrade within 190 days.

For the millions of Americans who feel cruddy every time they throw away a plastic fork, the marketing is absolutely baked into this product idea. And the sales show it, which is amazing—especially considering Eco-Products forgot to tell the story in the product design. Besides an off-white color and a matte finish, there is nothing to distinguish the product from bad old plastic utensils. Which means there is no way for the consumer to easily distinguish the "good" fork. And there is nothing about the design that would begin a conversation. The idea and the process have baked in the marketing. But when the poor fork goes out alone into the world, it has no way to communicate its story.

The narrative is lost. The good news is Eco-Products has done the really hard part right, and the right industrial designer can do the rest.

RECIPE

Begin by thinking of yourself as a designer. Start by making a list of all the things you've designed. Some software? A new sales program? A distribution plan? A meal plan for the kids? As you broaden your definition of design, you strengthen your inner consciousness of yourself as a designer. You are a designer. Design is just a good plan, after all.

Do the Bruce. Don't just design what you see in your business. Design what you don't see. Design for the change. Plot out your business for the next ten years. For example, if you have a product and you know you will have to update it every two years, look at that cost as a whole, and begin to design a more flexible system that will allow you to make those changes better and cheaper. Do you have a couple of ideas already?

Look at your entire business and write down an inventory of all the potential positive and negative touch points: the product, the packaging, the shipping, the packaging the customer has to throw away, the old product in the trash or landfill, the website, the uniforms, the trucks, the customer service people. *Everything*. Pay special attention to the stuff you would rather not think about. The biggest opportunities lie here. Put this list aside for now. You have ideas, but you'll have even better ideas soon.

Twitter @Bakedin #Mau

RECOGNIZE THE ARTIFICIALITY OF THE CORPORATION

A corporation, after all, is little more than a figment of our imaginations. In one respect, it's a wall that defines inside and outside. It's important to knock down that wall and invite your customers in. Today, customers are coming into your business if you want them to or not. It's time to embrace them and make them part of the design of your success. Use this new transparency to bake your marketing right into your organization.

Patagonia has long been a model for how a company can be successful and responsible at the same time. A lifetime guarantee is probably one of the oldest ways to bake your marketing into your product. At the time Patagonia came out with this promise, however, such guarantees had been mostly forgotten in a world of planned obsolescence. Most companies are terrified to stand behind their product to this degree, but Patagonia isn't, and it has benefited in innumerable ways—not just with great customer loyalty but also by attracting the kind of customer that isn't out to abuse the policy, because to abuse the policy would be to abuse the relationship. Patagonia stands for a customer-company relationship that its customers value highly because they believe in the company's integrity and see that it pushes Patagonia into pursuing new means to do what it does in more responsible and sustainable ways. Patagonia's mission statement says it all: "Build the best product, cause no unnecessary harm, use business to inspire and implement solutions to the environmental crisis." This mission statement is pure baked-in marketing; this is a company all of its customers want to proselytize.

But Patagonia has never said it was perfect. In fact, quite the opposite; the company has spoken about what it would like to do better. And its customers are part of this conversation about improvement. Recently, in an effort to erase the imagined wall between the company and its customers, Patagonia has begun making public the production process for many of its most popular items and inviting customer feedback.

The site Patagonia created to do this is called the Footprint Chronicles. Customers can select a product and see its total environmental impact, including energy used, carbon dioxide and waste created, and distance traveled. It's not a rosy picture. The first shirt we looked at on the site generated 27 pounds of carbon dioxide to create it. We kept looking and found one that created 15 pounds of carbon dioxide, then finally found a T-shirt that got that number down to 3.5 pounds. Cool. Another reason to wear only T-shirts.

The site has been widely praised, but it has also been criticized as a marketing ploy. In our way of thinking, when a good company tries to do the right thing and bakes that right into the way it does business and speaks to its customers, people are going to spread the word. That's great marketing. But it's no ploy.

RECIPE

Humanize your business. Think about the ways we talk about issues in corporate America. What sorts of things do you speak of in less human, less fully honest terms? Something probably comes to mind. Is there a way to strip away this obscuring veneer and offer more transparency to your customers? "No" is probably your immediate answer, but keep thinking on it. Start by saying, "It could work if...." and see what ideas come to you. Imagine your competitive advantage if you were the only company in your space that could have the conversation with customers that everybody else is afraid to have.

Progressive Insurance shows its customers all of its competitors' insurance rates. It humanized the process and did something its competition would never do. What is your version of this?

Twitter @Bakedin #Human

GET OUT OF WHATEVER BUSINESS YOU THINK YOU'RE IN

In our digital age, technology is definitely making it more difficult to tell the difference between product and marketing. Is a website a product, a retail location, or marketing? The answer is *yes*. Those lines have blurred. And being on the right side of those blurred lines is important to success. Success starts by making it a habit to push against your definition of where the product begins and where it ends. Sometimes looking at something from a different perspective is all it takes to shift your conception of these things.

Early designers and makers of MP3 players thought of them in the context of the portable CD players that had come just before. The driving concept had been to make a smaller device that could hold a bunch of digitized CDs. And this they did. And MP3 players were selling very, very slowly because unless you were really tech savvy, you didn't know where to get these mysterious MP3 files to play on them. Steve Jobs and Apple saw the market through a different lens than the early MP3 player pioneers. Apple recognized the challenge—and in it, the opportunity—to develop a new standard of music, in which it could own the delivery of digital music as part of a whole new MP3 player system.

Apple realized that the product didn't end where everybody else thought it did. The early MP3 manufacturers all thought it stopped at the edges of the device, but in the case of the iPod, you plugged the device into another expression of the product— online. The device was seamlessly integrated into the organization and storage and purchase of digital content. Where does the iPod begin and end? Apple repeated the same process with the iPhone. Rather than try to create a marginal improvement on the cell phone concept, Apple took the bigger view, conceiving a new digital tool that can connect you with *everything*.

Every company has the ability to look with new eyes at its own history and the culture in which it exists. Are you in the sunglass business or the fashion accessory business? Are you in the coffee business or the meeting place business? Are you in the guitar business or the music performance business? Are you in the pen business or the personal expression business? Are you in the water business or the hydration business? Are you in the car business or the personal transportation business? (Somebody, please answer this one soon.) Constantly pushing to understand the potential boundaries of your product has become more important as consumer expectations have begun to push the boundaries of what was possible just a few short years ago.

Today, the question of "what is product?" is further blurred by the question of "what is work?" Think about it. You could work as a graphic artist and have a hobby rebuilding classic cars or, conversely, you could rebuild classic cars for a living and do graphic arts for a hobby. But which one is work and which is a hobby? It used to be that work was defined by what you did to make money, and yet, these days, people have begun to monetize their hobbies online by selling advertising on their blog or starting a store on eBay.

Photography is a great example of this paradigm shift. It used to be that professional photographers ruled the roost and used a handful of professional stock agencies to represent them. If you needed a photo for your magazine, ad, or brochure, you had two choices. You could either hire a photographer for several thousand dollars a day, or you could buy a one-time right to a photograph from one of the stock agencies for anywhere from hundreds to thousands of dollars.

Then, along came digital photography. Prior to that, shooting good photos was hard. You had to get the shot; but beyond that, there was no way to improve it if you made a simple mistake on the exposure. Now, every amateur photographer can take great photos with great tools. Photographers can see photos in real time and then make adjustments without burning expensive film. The new medium also gives amateurs the ability to learn faster and become better with every shot. But the biggest shift has come from programs like Photoshop. Now, instead of spending years learning the esoteric art of manipulating images in the darkroom, you can improve your photos with the click of a mouse.

Today, there are legions of amateur photographers who wouldn't mind making a few bucks from their hobby. iStockphoto.com has taken advantage of the trend. Bruce Livingstone, an amateur photographer who simply wanted to share his photos with his friends, started the company in 2000. Now, iStockphoto, the first Internet-based, member-generated image and design community, has more than three million photographs for sale, created by hundreds of thousands of amateur photographers who, like Bruce, did not want a job as a photographer but simply wanted to make a little extra money to pay for their habit. Bruce's idea caught on. In 2006 iStockphoto was sold to Getty Images for more than $50 million. Not bad for an amateur working on his hobby.

It's ironic that while the root of the word "amateur" comes from "amor" or "to love"; amateurs are usually seen as second-class citizens to the professionals. Today, the lines have blurred. Now, if you love to do something—whether it's your hobby or your work— you are, by definition, an amateur. With the new tools of co-creation, more people now have the power to do what they love *and* earn money doing it.

RECIPE

Find out what business you're in. Start by writing down what business you *thought* you were in. Below it, write down all the services you provide people by being in the business you thought you were in (make sure to focus on the moments in your professional experience you've enjoyed the most). Finally, make a list of the emotional benefits you provide to your customers.

Is it possible, as you look at all of these things, that you'll see you're actually in a much more potentially interesting business (or businesses) than you originally thought? Does this new perspective on what you actually provide have implications for the things you do and make? How can you use this new perspective to design a new offering for your customers?

Twitter @Bakedin #Newbiz

UNDERSTAND BOTH SIDES OF YOUR TRUTH

Many companies have forgotten the truth of what their product is all about. Dig into your organization's culture. Find out what your customers think. Diagnose everyone's various sacred cows. Then, flip it all over and look at it again; you might find the truth (or a new truth) in what you thought was impossible. Innovation from the top down and from the inside out is being flipped on its head, as we know; however, it must still be supported and nurtured from the top down. With the right encouragement, innovation can spring from anywhere.

The North Face brand has been able to stay relevant to the core outdoor sports market even as it has become mainstream. It's done this by tapping into the deep culture of people who usually disdain the mainstream. It has done this by keeping a team of climbers, skiers, snowboarders, and endurance runners involved with the brand. While most brands might pay lip service to their sponsorships of athletes, the North Face has made them the centerpiece of its product design and marketing efforts. The company also fosters its reputation for staying genuine and relevant by funding expeditions. In these respects, it has allowed the company's core customers to play a major role in shaping the brand's story and aligning its marketing and product design. This has allowed traditional customers to feel connected to the core of the brand, while still allowing the brand itself to expand beyond the outdoor industry.

The hardcore athlete is key to success in the outdoor industry. This is true. But the leaders of one little-known company are finding success by flipping that truth to find truth in the inverse. The people at the clothing company Nau realized that the entire industry had focused on the heroic accomplishments of extreme athletes instead of the experiences that we all have access to in the outdoors. Hal Arneson, Nau's creative director, shared a few thoughts with us about how Nau had decided to flip that truth to find its own unique voice—one that informed everything it does, from product design to marketing:

> The model for marketing success in the outdoor industry has long been one of hero worship, centered on peak activities performed by elite athletes. The athletes and the activities

themselves are elevated to mythical status, and the featured product is valued in part because it is perceived to be built to withstand the rigors of these extreme situations, but mostly because the purchaser feels that by wearing the same product as the rock star, surf god, or paddling diva who wore that product in the magazine, they would, by association, be perceived as being capable of the same feats.

There's a new paradigm forming, one in which the aspirational model becomes more about the experience and less about the personality. In place of these sport-specific uberathletes, the new role models are those individuals who understand their athleticism as just one part of what makes them who they are, who don't simply recreate, but are acutely aware of the environment that sustains this recreation. They are multi-sport, multi-season athletes who understand the value in matching their activities to the conditions that exist and the opportunities that are available.

Our participation in the outdoors extends beyond the sports we do. Simply being out there invites an awareness of the fragile ecosystems that exist, and our responsibility to protect them for future generations. The new paradigm is one of a larger, more conscious view of the outdoor experience and how it fits into all aspects of one's life. A view that includes the peak moments as well as the mundane, one that moves between trail and town, between hard core and hanging out.

It's time to align ourselves with the values that draw us to the outdoors, rather than with the high-profile personalities who excel in only one small aspect of the larger outdoor experience.

This attitude of focusing on experiences versus accomplishments can extend well beyond the confines of the outdoor business. Think about new media and how it is affecting marketing. It's all about your willingness to experience the changes affecting how your company relates to its customers. You can either sit at the edge of the stream and notice which way the water is flowing, or you can jump into the stream and be a part of the currents flowing through our culture. It's only by jumping in that you start to feel the pull of the water and realize it isn't always going in the same direction. There is more than one truth to the flow of the stream.

You have to *live* your products and services to find these truths and inverted truths. It's simple: Use your company's products and services. Become a customer yourself. Every day, we hear stories about the out-of-touch executive. A few years ago, a story floated around that the top few hundred GM executives got their cars delivered to them, and thus never experienced the process of buying a car. It wasn't that surprising, but what a shame. In big companies, it's probably impossible to test-drive every product individually. The only way around that is to get everyone involved. Start using your products yourself, but more important, make doing so a part of your organization's culture. It should be common practice to call your own customer service department or work on the floor of your own stores. But to know even more truths, start using your competitors' products and services, too—especially those of your smallest competitors. And don't rationalize away what you learn. Find the truth they are exploiting that you are not.

Again, focus groups can be an obstacle in this respect—it's like they have become a weird simulacrum for actually spending time with customers. Sure, focus groups can yield fast feedback: You just pop into a room and watch them interact from behind a one-way mirror. (Faster yet, just read the report.) But how can you understand how your customers really live and think when you're trying to evaluate what a small group of them say while stuck in a sterile room, removed from the context of their daily lives?

Patrick J. Cescau, the CEO of Unilever, has solved this problem in a creative way. He commutes once a week between Unilever's U.K. headquarters and its global headquarters, which is an hour away. He hires a van, recruits a few customers, and does his own shop-alongs at the grocery store. Instead of sitting in focus groups or looking at a bunch of data about customers, he's out there interacting with them.

RECIPE

Make a systematic plan to get to know your entire business category so well that you can identify the two sides to any truth. Start by making sure you're using your own product. Then begin to use your competitors' products. Don't accept help that would be above or beyond what your average customer would get. Make this effort a part of every week—and don't allow it to be pushed aside.

Draw a line down the center of a page. On the left side, begin a list of the truths surrounding your product and your industry. On the other side of the line, write down all the ways in which you have seen the exact opposite to be true, either in your category or in another. What if you began to design for the right side of the line? What would be the opportunity? How would that change your products or services?

Twitter @Bakedin #Truth

TRUTH | OTHER TRUTH

GET YOUR HIVE ON

We've all seen that organizations can do some very dumb things, despite being filled with very smart people. There are a lot of reasons for this, but to put it simply, an organization has an IQ, and it's not equivalent to the CEO's IQ. Nor is it automatically the equivalent of senior management's average IQ. The intelligence of the whole can differ wildly based on who is connected to whom and how. If smart people in senior management are disconnected from the people in the trenches, the organizational IQ suffers. If brilliant middle managers are disconnected from the boardroom, the organizational IQ suffers.

The idea of an organizational IQ is one you don't hear very often, but the benefits of collaboration and networking are, of course, well known. Perhaps the best representation of this idea isn't found in even the most progressive corner of corporate America but rather in nature—bees. Individually, they aren't very bright creatures. It's estimated that each individual bee has only about a million cerebral nerve cells. But when combined, a bee colony has about 100 billion neurons. How many is that? Well, humans have 200 billion neurons, so a beehive might be about half as smart as you. And we see that in action. Bees make honey. (Do *you* know how to make honey?)

Somehow, in the environment of the hive, this simple animal contributes to some very sophisticated thinking about strategies for food gathering and defense. And they do it because every bee in the hive knows everything that is going on. Until recently, zoologists believed that during the famous tail dance, only those bees directly surrounding the dancing bee would be informed about a source of nectar. But recently, researchers found that the dance is actually a more refined form of communication. The collector bee's foot stamping and howling wing noise produce vibrations in the wax of the hive, transmitting the information to other collector bees throughout the hive.

"Bees use the hive as a sort of radio transmitter for important announcements," says neurobiologist Jürgen Tautz in his book *The Buzz About Bees*. Thus, a hive of bees is capable of making honey, although no single bee fully understands the whole process. And they don't need to, because a key feature of hive intelligence is task specialization. A task-specialized group requires a well-developed means of communication to work together effectively. Only by specializing tasks and communicating effectively can bees make honey, and make it quickly.

If this doesn't sound like your company, well, it should. The good news is that technology is making a new kind of hive intelligence available to humans, too. It's probably not a coincidence that Oracle named its new collaboration software Beehive. The simplest, fastest way to make an entire organization smarter is for every member to know what is going on. Technology has made it possible to communicate quickly throughout an entire organization, as well as to subsets within the organization. Specialization means that not everybody has to know everything. But when it comes to hive intelligence, it's better to communicate too much than too little. The system will balance itself over time, but it's best to start by overcommitting to communication.

RECIPE

Start by connecting departments, but don't stop there. Connect relevant departments with one another so they can oversee what the others are up to. Create lots of group e-mail lists for each of the departments, but then allow anybody within the organization to subscribe (and make it absolutely mandatory for managers to subscribe). Make sure everybody has a networked smart phone. Communication should be bee-like—by that we mean no long-winded multiparagraphed missives. Short and sweet questions and rapidly exchanged answers are the keys to hive intelligence.

Also, be sure to go beyond just e-mail. Use instant messaging, and even social networks like Facebook and Twitter. The more communication, the better.

Twitter @Bakedin #Hive

KNOCK DOWN THE WALLS

For many organizations, it's not that they lack great innovative ideas, or even the will to be innovative; rather, the internal silos and deadening process become roadblocks. These organizations create processes that become too institutionalized and too specialized, and eventually form rigid foundations that support silos. Marketing *can't* talk to finance. Finance *can't* talk to product design. Those days are gone. You've got to knock down the walls and get everyone collaborating.

Our friend Mike told us a great story that illustrates this point. He's in charge of marketing innovation for a large brewer, and he's a master at getting out on the streets and talking to people. A couple of years ago, while he was checking out the bar scene in New York City, he noticed an emerging theme—a lot of bars were serving sake-infused drinks.

He started to investigate sake further and found out a few interesting things. First, there was no national sake brand. Instead, the category was dominated by Japanese imports. Second, sake is made using the same brewing process as beer, the biggest difference being the use of rice instead of hops in the brewing process. In many breweries, a few brewing kettles sit idle as demand fluctuates. The combination of market demand, no category leader, and manufacturing similarities pointed to a big opportunity for his brewery to dominate a category.

When Mike started to build a business plan for the opportunity, he started running into roadblocks. It seemed the company had a well-defined innovation process, run by the product design group and not connected to marketing. The process was based on a four-year time horizon. In the first year, many ideas are vetted using strict evaluation criteria. Once the five most promising ideas are identified in that first year, the next two years are used to develop product ideas and refined business plans. In the fourth year, the product judged to have the most potential out of the five is established for launch.

One of the reasons Mike was excited about the sake opportunity was that he saw a trend starting to emerge. If the brewery could jump on that trend-driven opportunity, it could establish a leadership position in what might be a hot new category. But the four-year process meant that to fast-track his idea, Mike would have to displace one of the other ideas already in the pipeline. And that would be an almost impossible task, considering all of the structure established around the idea pipeline. So Mike's sake idea was put on the shelf.

Sometimes, the very structures created to foster innovation can be what prevents you from being innovative. Inside organizations, there is often confusion as to why particular structures exist. While many see elaborate structures as useful frameworks within which to work, such structures must be seen and understood as foundations out of which creativity can blossom. Hence, the best structure is often the most minimal necessary to enable innovators to take advantage of fast-developing opportunities evolving from cultural shifts and changing consumer desires. More important, if you can knock down the walls between the internal silos, innovation can be accelerated dramatically.

RECIPE

One great way to start knocking down the walls is to make other people look good. If you have a hand in hiring, hire great people and get out of the way. It's fun to be with people who make you feel good, right? And if they make you *look* good, all the better. Find ways to make the folks you work with feel good. How can you be better and faster at giving them positive feedback and credit for their good work? Here are some ideas: learn how to listen better, and show more interest in what your colleagues have to say. The next great idea might be there, in one of your staff members, waiting for you to hear it.

Twitter @Bakedin #Walls

BECOME A SILO JUMPER

Be a jumper. What? Yeah, jump across the department silos.

There is always risk that comes with silo jumping. It's exciting and dangerous. You might get fired. Yeah, it's that dangerous. Because if you're spending a ton of time in another department and trying to break down silos, folks might think you're a traitor and suspect the worst. At the very least, they'll think you might be wasting time when you could be doing the same thing everyone else in the department is doing. So make sure you're taking care of business in your own silo. But sometimes the situation in an organization is desperate, and asking first doesn't always work very well. Take action. Sometimes it's hard to get permission to do extraordinary things, as Mike's story shows.

Go slowly, at first. It can be a bit like entering a foreign country. Everyone is a citizen of the same company, but not everyone shares the same language, let alone the same goals. They'll probably be a little suspicious of you. But—if we're right—*you're* a little suspicious, too. So smart silo jumpers actually start by inviting folks from other departments to jump into their meetings, too. Shake it up in your department by inviting strangers. You'll know things are starting to happen when the folks from other departments start asking you questions and inviting you to meetings. That'll make it official. You're a silo jumper.

RECIPE

When you're trying to figure out how to become a silo jumper, seek out the experts. They're the generalists. Generalists have made a career out of jumping from one silo to the next. In any company, the generalists are usually easy to spot. They're the ones whose career path hasn't been linear. They've been in marketing, on the product side, in sales, and maybe even in finance.

Usually, it's the generalists who can get things done. They know whom to ask to get involved in a project. They know where to turn for answers. As a bonus, they can make the mistake or ask the stupid question an expert might not be able to. And they're not expected to be right every time. Most important, they understand the unspoken system of how things get done. Can you spot the generalists? Seek them out, and start learning from them.

Twitter @Bakedin #Jumper

TAP THE UNTAPPED

Something happens after you've been at the same organization for a long time. You begin to believe your vision to the exclusion of all others. It can be a powerful force when you're starting out to forge your own unique perspective on things. And developing a unique vision and culture can be half the battle of achieving success. But at some point, a unique vision can mutate into narrow thinking and an insulated culture.

The best way to mitigate this is with constant

dosages of new blood, albeit in appropriate proportions. Outsiders are usually pretty ignorant about how things work in a company. That's *good*. That means—like the generalists—they can ask the sorts of questions other people in a company are unwilling to ask. They can talk about the elephant in the room without offending anyone. And often, they can see things that are impossible for a company's veterans to see.

Innovations usually happen at the intersection of disciplines, whether they are internal or external. This happens in science all the time. Dwayne Spradlin, CEO of InnoCentive, told us a wonderful story recently. Not too long ago, a drug company got an unusual toxicology result during a drug study. The best toxicologists inside the company couldn't understand the results. They turned to external academics, but they couldn't figure it out, either. Stumped, they turned to an open-source innovation company, InnoCentive.

InnoCentive was spun off from Eli Lilly as a way for companies to tap into the expertise of outside scientists to get fresh perspectives on innovation problems. After the drug company posted the problem that had stumped it for so long, an InnoCentive protein crystallographer looked at it. With one quick look, he noticed that a simple solution he used quite often in his own work could solve the problem.

The drug company was blown away. The people there had never viewed the problem as a crystallography problem; they saw it as a toxicology problem. By changing their perspective, they opened up a whole new way for the firm to solve problems and even shifted how they thought about the types of innovation challenges they face daily.

The same sorts of issues exist with internal silos, and even with internal incentives, that can get in the way of open innovation. If you can knock down the walls between your organization's internal silos and the outside community, you might find that innovation can be accelerated dramatically.

RECIPE

One of the keys to tapping untapped resources is to realize that the community around your products is bigger than your company. There are many passionate people who would love to help you improve your products and spread your marketing. It's important to remember that this community thrives on open dialogue. Hence, the walls of your company have to become porous.

Think about how you relate to people outside your company. Is your organization litigious or inviting? Can people at all levels of your organization dialogue with outsiders? Invite people to participate by communicating openly; write a blog, publish articles, give speeches, and publish information about projects on resources like InnoCentive. Focus on connecting and building community. Instead of dictating your vision, try listening and responding to what others think. When you invite dialogue, you'll be amazed by the kind of fresh perspective you'll gain and the kind of creative momentum you'll build.

Twitter @Bakedin #Tap

SACRIFICE AND SIMPLIFY

Jumping silos tends to be easier in a smaller company, which makes the process of baking in your marketing easier, too. Big companies tend to adopt an "iteration mode" toward product—small, incremental improvements to old ideas. In this model, the two most powerful words are "new" and "improved," but in the world of innovation, two of the most powerful words are "sacrifice" and "simplify." How can sacrifice and simplify beat new and improved? Because the sacrifice-and-simplify philosophy simply makes better products that consumers like more.

In the world of consumer electronics, a little company like Pure Digital would seem to be at a huge disadvantage in going up against some of the biggest brands in the world. Its category of choice, video cameras, seems fraught with insurmountable hurdles in terms of the pace of technology. How could it hope to compete?

Flip didn't even try. Instead, it created a whole new category of video cameras defined by two main features: (1) A built-in USB connection that allowed the camera to charge and download to your computer instantly, and (2) Nothing. No other features. That's right. At a time in the camera category when it was all about features and feature wars, Flip left all the other must-have features off its product—no zoom, no special effects, no light settings, and no flip-out screen. The list of what it doesn't have could fill the page. In fact, the Flip camera has a grand total of six buttons. It also just happens to be everything most people would ever need for shooting video. And it has been a sensation. Flip's company, Pure Digital, grew 44,667 percent in the last five years and has sold more than 1.5 million devices since it first unveiled its Flip product line in 2007. In fact, its momentum has been so significant that in 2009, Cisco decided to buy Pure Digital for $590 million.

But Flip didn't stop there. It just keeps on baking the marketing into its product. The digital video files the Flip generates can be shared easily enough, whether attached to e-mail or posted on sharing sites. The software that comes with the camera includes the simplest movie-making software imaginable. You can make a movie in a few minutes—including music and title sequences, with the option of placing the Flip logo at the end. After an experience this good, we assume we're not the only people who opted to put the logo on when we sent our new movie greeting cards and e-mails to friends. Each and every one of those movie greeting cards added up to the best commercial Flip could ever hope to produce— part family film, part product endorsement.

RECIPE

Think about the products your company is producing. Most of us are in the habit of thinking about new features we could or should add to those products. We spend a lot of time thinking about how products can satisfy the various needs of customers. That's the way most of us are used to thinking of innovation. Instead, think about what you could *take away* from your product. Make a list of your product's features, according to their importance to the customer. Now cross off all but the top five. What would it mean to sacrifice the rest? Does your product still work? In what respects does it work better?

Twitter @Bakedin #Sacrifice

DON'T PUT THE WORD INNOVATION ON BUSINESS CARDS

When faced with the need to innovate, many companies establish special units, or "skunk works," to be their innovation engines. Obviously, this only adds to the silo-rific character of their corporate cultures. This new silo of the chosen few innovators has all the secrets, leaving the rest of the company scratching their heads as to how they can help. This can give the very idea of innovation a detached, standoffish character.

The skunk works strategy is not only a potential demotivator for an organization's many other potential innovators, but it's also risky from a very pragmatic perspective. If the business experiences tough times at some point in the future, a special unit that's focused on innovation, and which might not be pulling in the same kind of revenue as other divisions, might be forced to shut down or scale back. *Poof*—innovation has just been removed from the company. Another practical risk is in having all of the big thinking locked up among a very select group of people who may not end up staying in the company. If you get raided, or they leave, so does the innovation practice.

The key is to embed innovation throughout all of the company's stakeholders, charging (and empowering) everyone from the CEO to the receptionists to the customers and even the investors to be more innovative as part of their daily routine. In this way, the inevitable ups and downs of your business will never disrupt its pipeline of great ideas.

In our ongoing search for worthy examples of who is doing innovation right, we love it when we find one that exists in a huge company. So often the game-changing work is happening with smaller companies. And we've all become guilty of thinking small means nimble and innovative, while large means slow and constipated. But Procter & Gamble (P&G) has been one of the leaders in shifting innovation into every corner of the organization and beyond. Historically, the mandate at P&G was to create its own innovation, internally, in its R&D practices. It was all very traditional. Likewise, P&G focused on its innovation prowess in the manufacturing and selling of its core products. Yet, as the innovation paradigm has shifted, P&G was one of the first to jump on the open-source innovation bandwagon.

The idea of open-source innovation comes from a very successful place: open-source software. Way back in the day, some smart individuals realized that they weren't as smart individually as everybody put together would be. This basic idea has worked many times over to help people solve software problems and bugs. And it's an idea that can and has been applied to all sorts of other areas, from mapping the craters of Mars by NASA to making a better mop.

To facilitate this transition, P&G started its Connect + Develop program. Here's what A.G. Lafley, the CEO and chairman of P&G said when he introduced the program on the company's website:

> Connecting with the world's most inspired minds. Developing products that improve consumers' lives. Our vision is simple. We want P&G to be known as the company that collaborates—inside and out—better than any other company in the world. I want us to be the absolute best at spotting, developing, and leveraging relationships with best-in-class partners in every part of our business. In fact, I want P&G to be a magnet for the best in class. The company you most want

> to work with because you know a partnership
> with P&G will be more rewarding than any other
> option available to you.

That's a pretty clear message coming from the head of P&G that innovation will not be the domain of a select few holed up in an ivory tower.

Connect + Develop should be viewed as P&G's co-creation manifesto. One of the most amazing aspects of the program is its holistic point of view. P&G invites everyone to be a part of its innovation conversation. It starts with the senior management, but it reaches out to every single employee in the organization. And it doesn't stop at the exterior walls. The conversation reaches out to partner companies, venture capitalists, and finally to P&G customers.

Everybody at P&G is probably scared to be inviting so many ideas and people and opinions into a process. How can the company retain control? Well, that only matters if control is the goal. But control isn't the goal—the goal is great, market-changing ideas. And you're going to have to give up some control to get that. That's an essential point of view when you're trying to create a new innovation culture in a huge company. Just keep telling yourself that if P&G can do it, you can do it.

In fact, perhaps the biggest opportunity that open-source innovation affords you is the ability to know your customers and their culture so much better. This knowledge will make it that much easier for you to use your own creativity and intuition to bake the marketing into your products.

RECIPE

Do you have an innovation department? Maybe you shouldn't. Try getting everyone involved in the process. Start by finding innovation evangelists in every department. Give them the task of getting others involved. Start an innovation movement. Make it contagious. Challenge people and award creativity. Ultimately, figure out a way make everyone in your organization accountable when it comes to innovation.

Twitter @Bakedin #100%

MINE YOUR HISTORY

Many companies forget what made them successful. A lot can be learned by simply mining the company's history through the lens of discovering inflection points for both products and marketing.

Every company has a grand story of how it was founded. For HP, it's the legendary garage. For Nike, it was Phil Knight, the waffle iron, and selling running shoes out of his station wagon. For Johnson Controls, it was Mr. Johnson inventing the thermostat. As companies get busy, the import behind those founding stories can be lost. They need to be mined as a source of inspiration and even guidance when it comes to defining the company's identity. Most often, rediscovering that original vision—which is usually steeped in product and not marketing—can be the start of creating a deeper brand narrative.

The term "brand DNA" refers to this early history. Violating those original missions and values can be perilous. It doesn't mean you shouldn't innovate and grow. Not at all. Rather, doing so helps create innovation by pointing up the consistent strategies and ideals that have led your company to success. You should demand that the same mission be applied to today's marketplace and consumer.

When we first started working with Domino's, the company's managers fondly remembered the good old days of the 30-minute guarantee. Back then, Domino's owned the delivery pizza category. It pushed its process to make pizza delivery into the most reliable delivery service around. It also developed a playful narrative that began every time a customer picked up the phone to place an order. It was a race: Would Domino's make the delivery in time? The race was full of drama and tension, keeping customers engaged.

Well, like many another great narratives, this one was stopped by a lawsuit after an accident involving a Domino's delivery person. The lawyers descended like vultures on a roadside pepperoni pizza. For years, people lamented the loss of the Domino's 30-minute guarantee. It was in the Domino's brand DNA, but it was off-limits.

Then, in the fall of 2007, Domino's reconnected with its DNA by flipping the promise on its head. Instead of the 30-minute guarantee, the paradigm was flipped to "You've got 30 minutes." The reclaiming of "30 minutes" could reconnect Domino's to its own history, while also leading the company to connect with consumers in a new way. At the time of the original 30-minute guarantee, the ordering technology available was basically a rotary phone. Today, innovation can be powered by the original promise of best-in-class delivery experience. This narrative can help define a vision not only for marketing but also for products.

Enter the Pizza Tracker. Consumers get stressed about their orders as soon as they hang up the phone. Why? Given today's technology, why not make the whole process transparent? Pizza Tracker is an online tool that shows you exactly where your pizza is, from the time the order is put in until it reaches your home. Pizza Tracker automatically launches with the online order, which is done with Pizza Builder—a big, visual interface that allows you to see what kind of pizza you're getting as you make your selections. Choose pepperoni and you see them get flipped onto your "pie." People who order online now consistently report higher satisfaction scores for both the service and the pizza than those who order the old-fashioned way.

So are Pizza Tracker and Pizza Builder marketing or product? YES.

It's comforting to sit at your desk and pretend to understand your brand and its customers from the inside out. Sure, it's great to understand the quantitative nature of what's happening in a business. But we too often forget that a brand is something alive in the culture at large, and not just inside the walls of an office. A brand is a conversation that happens in large part outside your company's walls. Even the brand DNA lives beyond the walls of the company. (In some cases, that might be the *only* place it still lives.) So to find out who you are, you've got to be where that conversation is happening. This requires interacting with people in a way that helps you not only to know what your brand conversation means out in the culture, but how you can get ahead of that conversation and anticipate its next steps. This will allow you to drive innovation from a place grounded in your brand's history.

PIZZA

RECIPE

Do you know your company's founding story? Some are about the place. Some are about the iconoclastic founder betting everything. Some are about overcoming great odds. These stories are always inspiring and can ground and clarify your thinking about the future. Also, think about the best product your company ever produced. Tell that story. Or the best marketing your company has done. What made it great? Share these stories, and explore what can you learn from them.

Twitter @Bakedin #DNA

FEELING CONFLICTED? GOOD.

Conflict. That's what we're always trying to avoid, isn't it? Yet conflict is what makes something stand out. Without it, a story doesn't work. It's what makes a product unique.

Companies are full of conflicts. They are usually those things buried deep inside a company that no one will ever talk about. In a very few cases, entrepreneurs who know how to use it will wield conflict as a powerful tool. While many companies try to make their brand or product relevant to a culture, most successful brands actually transform culture by finding and exploiting cultural conflicts and tensions, using them as a lever to drive change.

That's what happened at Nike. A few of the designers in that company's Innovation Kitchen started looking at the history of running injuries and noticed something interesting. The running shoe category had become all about injury prevention. Do you pronate or do you supinate? What shoe do you need to correct which problem and stabilize your foot? Over time, as running shoe companies put more and more money into R&D to prevent injuries, something very interesting happened. Nothing. Running injuries per thousand stayed relatively flat, even with all this focus on protection and prevention. The more effort shoe companies put into improving the way shoes corrected pronation, supination, forefoot bruising, and plantar fasciitis, to name a few, the less any of it worked. It was a dirty little secret that no one wanted to talk about.

What happened? First, Nike acknowledged that shoes aren't really built for feet. They're built for lasts. Lasts are the models shoes are built around. Sure, lasts *look* like feet. But lasts *aren't* feet, and they haven't really changed very much over the last hundred years or so. Second, Nike developed the theory that by building shoes with ever more protective features, the shoes were actually making people's feet weaker over time. With all of that protection, the foot muscles didn't have to work, and the tiny muscles that provide natural stability were starting to atrophy. Finally, Nike noticed that people who ran barefoot seemed to have *fewer* injuries. Yes, fewer injuries. So realizing all of this—and understanding that, originally, running shoes were made to provide protection from surfaces, but not to provide extra stability—Nike asked a question: What if we went back to the beginning and made a simple shoe that protected feet from surface wear and tear but let the foot operate freely?

Nike Free was born.

Nike Free is a niche product, at best. Nike has had the courage to allow and support a few rogue creators to question everything and create a product that calls into question everything else it does. Unfortunately, that story was disconnected from how the shoe was marketed. It may have seemed too risky to follow through on it. Nike Free probably would have been a better idea for a small company dead set on reinventing the entire category. But today, everyone needs to live by the motto, "It's better to destroy the current paradigm in which your products exist than let someone else do it." It sounds easy, but it takes a lot of guts.

RECIPE

Someone inside your company needs to be asking the biggest of questions. Like, does our core product really work? What would happen if we went in the exact opposite direction? What would happen if we tried to destroy ourselves? Will these kinds of questions produce conflict? You should hope so. There is a lot of power in conflict. Think about the categories you work in and the conflicts that exist among them. If you're in the traditional energy business, it's pretty obvious that you have a conflict with the environmental movement. If you're in the financial world, there's a lot of conflict around public trust. The cultural conflicts in your category are probably a bit subtler. What are the big, hairy cultural conflicts affecting your company that everyone knows about but no one really likes to discuss?

We always look for conflicts at CP+B. Whether it's helping MINI launch in the U.S. when SUVs dominated the market; or helping Burger King focus on a segment of the fast-food market that unapologetically wants indulgent food, while the culture at large is very concerned with fast food's impact on health. Unleashing the power of conflict can not only differentiate your products but also help them find the space to grow.

Twitter @Bakedin #Conflict

THE ALL-MIGHTY CO-CREATOR

As a culture, we have very romantic visions of the lone creative figure, that singular genius standing against all odds to see his or her vision through or die trying. Like Howard Roark, the architect hero of Ayn Rand's *The Fountainhead*, who chooses to blow up his own building rather than see his design vision compromised. It's these notions that make it so hard to loosen our chokehold on the innovation process. But creativity and innovation are so important to solving our problems, both big and small, that we can't let mythology stand in our way.

Co-creation can mean a lot of different things. But at its most basic, it just means *help*. Help create. Maybe it's something simple like a bunch of kids around a table with Levi Strauss designers, throwing around ideas for new jeans. Or maybe it's the idea of letting customers pick the image on your label each month. Either way, the concept is the same. The only way to start is to loosen up on the reins and see where it takes you. To be a mighty co-creator, you have to put your fear aside and get your control freak on lockdown.

The good news is you will have lots of new friends because these days everyone wants to be a creator. But they'll settle for being a co-creator with you. They want to be involved in the products they buy. And if you don't let them in, they'll still be involved—but probably in ways that are a lot less positive for your company. Maybe they'll dog out your product via consumer reviews and social networks. They have energy—and it's up to you to channel it into something positive. Your harshest critics often become your best collaborators and your biggest fans.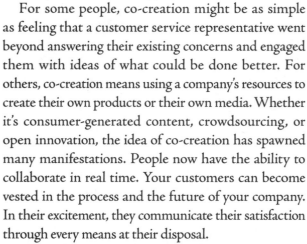

For some people, co-creation might be as simple as feeling that a customer service representative went beyond answering their existing concerns and engaged them with ideas of what could be done better. For others, co-creation means using a company's resources to create their own products or their own media. Whether it's consumer-generated content, crowdsourcing, or open innovation, the idea of co-creation has spawned many manifestations. People now have the ability to collaborate in real time. Your customers can become vested in the process and the future of your company. In their excitement, they communicate their satisfaction through every means at their disposal.

Although the tools of co-creation have changed many industries, making companies more open to customer input and innovation, there's still a pervasive feeling that the experts inside a company are always right. They are the professionals. Michael Treacy, author of a 2005 article in *Advertising Age* entitled Ignore the Consumer, loudly echoed this sentiment:

> Companies spend billions on market research to divine the needs and wants of consumers and businesses. Yet the new-product failure rate remains high. And we're not coming up with better product concepts by listening to the voice of the customer. Why? Maybe the customer isn't worth listening to.

Amen, brother. But while we appreciate Treacy's point of view, and we have *definitely* seen bad research used as a proxy for listening, it isn't the customers that actually lead an innovation effort astray. It's not listening that's a problem but *how* we listen. Just like people, some companies are good listeners, and some are bad listeners.

We've spent enough time inside companies to see how well they do or don't listen to consumers, and more often than not, bad research is used as an excuse to minimize risk and minimize innovation. Too many times, it's internal agendas and politics and misuse of consumer research that get in the way of true innovation. (It's also worth noting that consumer research is a lot different from co-creation—as different as if we asked you to fill out a form about what it's like to push a car out of a ditch or instead had you help us push the car out of the ditch.)

While we can all point out innovations in marketing and product design that sprang from the brilliance of one mind, the truth is that most innovation happens when co-creation is at the center of the innovation process. This usually means involving not only the internal resources of the company and a team charged with innovating—whether it be product or marketing—but also the external resources available from your customers and the broader culture.

There is no formulaic way to do this; the key is simply taking a more holistic, inclusive approach that doesn't exclude potential input—especially that of your customers. When inclusive dialogue is at the creative center of your brand's product and marketing narratives, powerful things happen. Instead of trying to manage your company's relationship with its customers and their culture, think instead about being their voice inside the walls of your company. Allow members of your brand's community, both inside and outside the company, to take self-guided explorations.

Threadless is a great example of this. The company started in 2000 with $1,000 of seed money from the founders, Jake Nickell and Jacob DeHart. By now, Threadless has redefined what it means to be a customer-focused company. It's at the forefront of the whole concept of baking the marketing into the product and getting customers involved in the process.

More than a company, Threadless is a community facilitator. Community members upload their T-shirt designs to the Threadless website, where visitors and other members of the community score them on a scale of 0 to 5. On average, around 700 designs compete in any given week. Each week, the staff then selects about ten designs for actual production based on the community's feedback—and those T-shirts are then sold off the Threadless site. Everyone whose design is selected receives $2,500 in cash. While lots of companies think about and even say they have formed a community around their products, they haven't put the community of customers at the center of their business the way Threadless has.

After so much success with Threadless, Jake Nickell is now putting the things he's learned about building communities to use in launching other companies through skinnyCorp (parent company)—like Naked&Angry, which uses a similar approach to textile patterns and designs and applies them to products like dishes, wallpaper, purses, and on and on.

As we all first learned in navigating the waters of our early romantic relationships, you can participate in and perhaps guide a relationship, but you certainly can't control it. Engaging in a community, it turns out, is a lot like dating. At first, people are giddy to be involved. After a while, the human ups and downs of relationships begin to emerge, and the giddiness is joined by less positive feelings, like insecurity and disappointment. Experiencing those feelings, though, is all part of being in a relationship. To gain the most from a community, you've got to be committed in good times and in bad.

We had an illuminating experience with Shure. A couple of years ago, John bought a pair of Shure E3 earbud headphones. Over the next year, his earbuds failed twice. While Shure's customer service staff was fine about replacing them, after they failed for the third time, John realized that no matter how good Shure's customer service process was, the product experience was unreliable. After all of the hassles, he wasn't sure he wanted to be a Shure customer anymore. John just wanted his money back. So, as a last-ditch effort, he put a call into Patrick Kilroy, Shure's VP of global marketing and left a message explaining the problem.

To John's surprise, his cell phone rang at around seven the next morning. It was Patrick Kilroy. Pat said he wanted to solve the problem John had called about the day before. On the call, he introduced John to Scott Sullivan, Shure's senior director of product development for personal audio products. Pat explained to John that he had only been at Shure for two weeks, and Scott had a lot more experience to solve John's problem. Shure listened, and John loved it. After that experience, John became a missionary for the brand, telling his story over and over.

RECIPE

Look around. Are your customers demanding more involvement in your brand and with your products? Are they talking about your products on blogs and other social media? The first step in your exploration of this opportunity is to get into the conversation. Start answering questions about your products on Facebook, Twitter, and other social media. Make comments on relevant blog posts. Likewise, ensure that your website is more interactive. Let people leave comments on it, and make sure they're answered.

The key is the ability to engage, to be involved in dialogue. It's a hard shift to make from inside-out to outside-in innovation—but most likely, it's inevitable. Once you get the hang of participating in an open flow of conversation, millions of possibilities unfold. You can start getting feedback from the community you've engaged, in ways that might complement or even replace customer service or market research. Once you've built the dialogue, you've created the conduit through which ideas can really start to flow. People *want* to participate. But remember, the only way to keep ideas flowing is to keep the dialogue going.

Twitter @Bakedin #Co-creation

FEEL IT IN YOUR BONES

How much do you use your intuition? Probably more than you think. It's a key ingredient in the baked-in process. Unfortunately, over the past couple of decades there has been a big push toward quantifiable analytics in business; the mantra is, "If it isn't measurable, it doesn't exist." This idea rules out intuition as a component of success—yet over and over we come across successful people who credit intuition as the key to their results. Not everybody has great instincts, and in all probability, the rise of quantifiable analytics was powered by those poor souls who need a way to navigate business without it. Well, we'd never deny the existence of analytics, but we're here to argue that you can go the other way, too. If your intuition isn't rippling with muscle, there are things you can do to make it stronger.

The old rule was to use competitive business analysis to drive innovation. Strategic planning was based on economic theory using data, demographics, your own company's economic situation, and your competitors' comparable information.

Today, a new body of evidence shows that while these predictive models might give us a sense of security, most real innovation comes from the power of randomness. Nassim Nicholas Taleb writes on page 38 in *The Black Swan: The Impact of the Highly Improbable:*

> It is high time to recognize that we humans are far better at doing than understanding, and better at tinkering than inventing. But we don't know it. We truly live under the illusion of order believing that planning and forecasting are possible. We

are scared of the random, yet we live from its fruits. We are so scared of the random that we create disciplines that try to make sense of the past—but we ultimately fail to understand it, just as we fail to see the future.

Random tinkering is the path to success. And fortunately, we are increasingly learning to practice it without knowing it—thanks to overconfident entrepreneurs, naive investors, greedy investment bankers, confused scientists and aggressive venture capitalists brought together by the free-market system.

For many of the analytical people of the world, that's not very comforting. Yet paradigm-shifting innovations such as Post-its, cellophane, Teflon, and Scotchguard emerged out of experimentation and intuition, not from a strategic innovation process based on a specific plan. Instead of a scientific "Eureka!" moment, these innovations are often expressed with a sense of surprise—more of a "huh?" moment, or perhaps a "what the...?" moment.

If the world is way more unpredictable than we all think it is, what do we do? The key lies in intuition. But intuition can be a hard thing to embrace in a business setting. Who wants to admit to relying on something like intuition when it comes to important marketing and product decisions?

huh?

what the...?

Look around. Innovation has become more of an all-or-nothing game. Brands that are built on intuition are more likely to be disruptive, and to adapt to and capitalize on a rapidly changing and unpredictable environment. Conversely, many aging brands have struggled because they have been unable to innovate and renew themselves. Sometimes that means irrelevant products, brands, or even whole business structures need to die for something else to thrive. Intuition can fuel this process of inspiration, competition, and cultural renewal.

Often, intuition is seen as that hunch or that gut feeling you have about something. While ordinary intuition may work in your day-to-day life, design intuition is a little different, and it's what drives good innovative decision making. Think of design intuition as a tool to translate experiences into action by marrying rational thinking with the emotional feelings that arise when facing a problem you haven't faced before. To be effective, design intuition should be rooted in reality, logic, knowledge, and experience.

In the world of business, Steve Jobs has exhibited an incredible ability to use design intuition to produce paradigm-shifting products like the iPod and iTunes. It was Jobs's deep knowledge of the computer business and empathy for users that allowed him to make the leap from the MP3 players available on the market at the time to the iPod. Jobs has always had a knack for deeply understanding the culture, applying that knowledge to the external circumstances facing Apple, and coming up with powerful solutions to business and product problems.

Design intuition, as we see it, is what really separates those who are good at innovating products and marketing from those who are great. But it takes courage, as design intuition is at its core about moving forward into an unknown future.

Too many design-planning processes become an exercise in making a product more likeable. Such incremental improvement can't really be called innovation. Great brands that are culturally relevant are built on the kind of intuition that gives a brand the ability to leapfrog the competition and change the game, the way Google, Amazon, and Threadless have done.

RECIPE

Making intuition a more powerful innovation tool comes with practice. Everyone has the ability to be an intuitive designer; we just need to do some training. Start by integrating design intuition into all of your decisions by starting off with the question, "What if...?" Once you start exercising your strategic intuition muscles, you'll be able to recognize important patterns. The more you train, the more patterns you recognize.

Also, encourage others to use their design intuition. It's contagious and inspiring. Ask them to dig deeper into how they *feel* about a design or marketing insight. Where would they take it? For many, intuition can be a particularly hard thing to express, and it's the sort of quality many people don't feel confident expressing. Help make sure people's intuitive thinking is supported and not quashed by overanalysis. Be positive. Welcome heresy.

Twitter @Bakedin #Bones

STEAL TO INNOVATE

T. S. Eliot once wrote, "Immature poets imitate; mature poets steal." Companies that simply imitate other products constantly find themselves two steps behind their competitors. The key to stealing innovation is to steal it from a different place altogether, a place outside of your competitive set. If you try to steal from inside your category, you're actually doing just the old-fashioned, regular form of stealing, and that will land you in court or jail. Stealing to innovate requires piecing together different elements, essentially, to create something new.

This may seem like a controversial idea, but look around. You'll see that some of the strongest companies "stole" their ideas. Apple "stole" Xerox's graphical user interface and mouse ideas. Facebook and MySpace "stole" Friendster's social network idea. Microsoft "stole" Netscape's browser idea. Nikon and Canon "stole" Kodak's idea for digital photography. The list goes on and on. No matter the industry, it always seems like the originator of an idea never becomes the dominant player in the long run. Often, the idea or innovation might be powerful, but ahead of its time. In most cases, it needs to be tweaked and massaged before it becomes a hit. While the idea is cool, we still don't see many flying cars in the sky. No doubt someone will figure out a way to make the idea happen. Maybe T. S. Eliot's quote can be restated here, "Immature innovators imitate; mature innovators steal." They take the opportunity to seize an idea and use it to create a new product.

RECIPE

What have you stolen lately? Is there something a competitor does that you could do better? Is there a new process or product that could be disruptive in your market, but isn't quite dialed yet? What can you do to make it more relevant? Nikon and Canon embraced the idea of replacing film with a digital sensor, taking the idea of a digital camera to places Kodak could never go with its heritage in film. It's our belief that good ideas are easy to come by. Where the hard work happens is in the process of making these ideas relevant. Steal good ideas. Make them relevant to your products. You'll be able to stay ahead of the competition.

Twitter @Bakedin #Steal

TAKE A FEARLESS APPROACH

A fearless approach can furnish you and those around you with the confidence to innovate, especially in this era of uncertainty. Yet, in a world where the greatest brands can fall by the wayside in an instant, there is no choice. Being fearless doesn't mean being irrational or completely without fear. Fear is part of being human. The key is being able to distinguish sensible fear from fear that's just a human reaction inhibiting your ability to be bold, dynamic, and innovative.

One tactic for dealing with fear is to move it a bit, relocating it relative to where you are. We've found that fear often attaches itself to random things or experiences. Fear happens, and it either grips you and holds you or you watch it pass through. If you can do the latter, you'll still be noticing your fear, but at more of a distance. "Oh, I'm afraid of this. How interesting. Let me examine that." Acknowledge the fear, learn what you can do about it, and continue on your course.

Considered practically, fear can help fuel you. A friend of ours used to say, "Why are so many people afraid of so many things, but they're never afraid of mediocrity?" Well, the reality is that most great innovators are afraid of exactly that. They don't want to pass through this life without leaving evidence that they were here. So if you have some fear and it's holding you back from living the life you want, having the job you want, and doing the things you want, why not consider flipping that fear from obstacle to fuel, so it actually goes to work for you?

Fear is also a wonderful marker. It will let you know when you are onto something truly new and fresh. We all share a tiny fear of the unknown. Experiencing fear in this context lets you know when you're going into a truly innovative space by firing off some butterflies or bristling those little hairs on the back of your neck. Respond to those sensations and get in the game.

Part of being fearless is being unfazed by the *idea* of failure. Notice that we say the idea of failure. Failure is often an idea—not an outcome—that stands in the way of success. It's something climbers have to think about all of the time. Some climbers begin to see falling in much the same way many business people see failure. Julian Saunders, a well-known Australian climber, gave this advice on how to improve climbing. It applies to innovation and business as well:

> FALL...a lot. The fear of falling is the biggest of all handbrakes that translates to a few things. Jump off at the anchors regularly if you are getting there without falling. If you are at all worried about falling, you will never try your hardest. You won't be focused on the next move, but rather on the fall. Then, you might as well just give up.
>
> TRY TRY TRY. Never say "take." Try until you

fall. And, when you think you are done and going to fall, try anyway. You'll be surprised (I guarantee it) how many times you will go through to the top. Not to mention, you will generally just be happier with your effort. It becomes more memorable. It's especially difficult to convince yourself to do it at the time, because the chance of falling in your own head is almost a given. So you think about that instead. It's easier to say take down or climb down, but you are usually underselling your capacity. Back yourself with the might of a nuclear warhead. Climbing a more difficult route than you think you can is more about trying than training.

It turns out falling isn't failing—falling is just part of succeeding. And in innovation, the falling—or the idea of failure—that most people are trying to avoid is *being wrong*. None of us wants to be wrong, but to innovate you have to get comfortable with being wrong. It takes a thousand or maybe a million wrong ideas to make a great innovation truly right. Let it happen. You have to create a culture where being wrong (falling) is just part of the process of succeeding.

RECIPE

How does your company deal with failure? Is it celebrated as an inevitable part of innovation, or is it seen as something to be avoided at all costs? Usually, fearless leaders provide inspiration for fearless companies. That doesn't always mean the founder or CEO could be a group leader or the leader of a division. Think about whether you are or your company is fearless. Can you move at lightning speed to address a change in the marketplace? Are you willing to risk being wrong to get to market first with an idea? Becoming more fearless is a learned skill that only comes through failing. The old innovation expression, "fail fast," is more important than ever these days as our world speeds up.

Twitter @Bakedin #Fearless

BE A HERETIC

The term "heretic" has always had religious connotations, as it refers to someone whose opinion is a deliberate departure from accepted church doctrine. The business world needs more heretics. The marketplace needs more people who see outside the standard paradigm in an industry and have the courage to change it.

The standard paradigm represents the usual way to get things done. It's easy—but is it any damn fun? Look around. Innovation always happens at the edges, the outer boundaries, where someone uses intuition to break with the standard paradigm and do something different.

Dick Fosbury shocked the track-and-field world in 1968 by high-jumping upside down. Instead of following the standard paradigm and jumping stomach first over the bar, he jumped back first. Fosbury was rewarded with Olympic gold and broke the Olympic record. Such gains don't come from following the crowd. Now everybody jumps upside down. Upside down has become the new right side up. But somebody is going to find a way to jumps sideways or feet first or back on the belly and go higher still. Will it be you?

In business, if you're a heretic in an established market, it usually means you've started a new one. Heretics are usually empowered by new technologies that at the time seem benign, but that can be highly disruptive to the established way of doing things. Amazon used the Internet to usher in its heresy. It's hard to believe that anyone questioned the idea of selling books online, but no one could see the power in the model way back in 1994 when Jeff Bezos started the company. Now Amazon is causing a stir with the Kindle 2's new Read-to-Me function. The idea of being able to shift between reading a book and listening to a book is pretty cool for tired eyes. But, as have most heretics, Amazon is being threatened with trial by fire from the Authors Guild. The Guild has said that the Read-to-Me function of the Kindle 2 violates copyright protection for audio versions of books.

While it might take a while to sort out the legal and ethical issues around the Kindle 2's new feature, it will only be a couple of years until the heretical nature of this technology is ubiquitous with every machine we interact with. Just look how fast photography has changed since the first digital cameras came on the market 18 years ago.

RECIPE

Being a heretic takes guts. It means not just going a different way from your competitors, but going a different way from the established norms within a whole culture. What's happening in the culture around your business? Is there something that's percolating outside the market that might cause radical changes to the way companies and customers interact? Amazon is just one of several disruptive examples that have destroyed existing ways of doing business. Can you take advantage of a disruptive technology that could, possibly, change the way you do your core business or service? Learn the new technology. Start applying it in small doses. If it works, flip the paradigm, lead the disruption, and be a heretic.

Twitter @Bakedin #Heretic

THINK BIG. THEN REALIZE THAT'S NOT BIG ENOUGH.

It's easy to get stuck in only seeing part of an opportunity to innovate. There are so many different factors involved that can cause your project to get knocked off the track or shot to the moon. Only by thinking holistically can you make an innovation truly succeed. Maybe the assignment is to create a new product for a category, when what is needed is a change in the way the product is communicated. Or it could be the other way around. Or more likely, it's both.

OXO makes kitchen tools. It understood that the market for kitchen tools could change. OXO recognized that kitchen tools on the market at the time were ugly, and felt this was an opportunity to do better. OXO did its job pretty well, but its products didn't inspire people to cook—just making a better-looking tool wasn't going to light up the market. The other part of OXO's big idea came from a place very far from fashion or design. It came from elderly customers. It seems the small handles on spatulas and cheese graters were difficult to hold and manipulate. Suddenly, the OXO designers had a mission that could instruct the form. By coming up with a powerful narrative built on making kitchen tools easier to hold, OXO's product design and marketing worked hand in hand to explode the kitchen utensil market. OXO's products were universally appealing because they responded to multiple issues of form, appeal, and utility. And OXO transformed kitchen tools from a commodity category to one driven by actual consumer preference and loyalty.

But this big thinking on top of big thinking strategy can't be a one-time event. Going forward, OXO will have to add new perspectives to its big ideas or risk becoming the new "higher-designed" commodity.

RECIPE

First, you have to think big. Really big. Then you have to sit back and think about all the ways your thinking isn't big enough. Shoot holes in it. Look at it from the customer's point of view. Look at it from an environmental point of view. Look at it from a need-based point of view. This is why collaboration is so powerful. Every collaborator comes with a new vantage point and, maybe, a better vantage point. Are you collaborating enough with other designers? With your customers? Even with your competitors?

Twitter @Bakedin #Big

THINK SMALL. THEN REALIZE THAT'S NOT SMALL ENOUGH.

Sometimes it can be the smallest insight that creates a paradigm shift. Those unforeseen insights that nobody else seems to notice are often where culture starts to change. Usually, it's the small things happening with consumer behavior in a related field that can make the biggest difference.

A few years ago, for instance, we noticed a rise in pet culture. Not only did more people own pets, but the relationship between owner and pet was changing as well. Pets had become more than pets—they had become companions. And with that change in status, people started taking much better care of their pets, buying them everything from health insurance to custom outfits. Pet owners' happiness became fueled, in part, by their sense of their pets' happiness.

At the same time, we noticed that a lot of people who owned Volkswagen Passat wagons also owned dogs. It was easy to see why. Wagons are the perfect dog vehicle. It seemed like an interesting opportunity. But after going out and really listening to dog owners, we realized there was an interesting tension when it came to new cars and dogs. If you're a dog owner, you know what we mean. While you might want a new car, you know your dog will soon make your new car look old with slobber, mud, and general dog wear and tear.

Instead of using advertising to convince dog owners that the Passat Wagon was the perfect vehicle for them, we felt it was much more powerful to come up with a Passat Wagon Dog Edition. The Dog Edition came with a special rubber insert that slides into the back of the Passat Wagon, filled with everything necessary to make the dog's life happier, including a dog ramp and a place for everything from a Frisbee to a blanket. We realized that a happy dog makes for a happy dog owner.

RECIPE

Are you thinking small enough? What's a niche in the market that seems to be forgotten by everyone else that you can own? Are there any small niche customers, like dog owners, with whom you can innovate? Also, think small when it comes to your products. How can you innovate a product feature that seems small but could do huge business? This is another reason why we like the new Amazon Kindle's Read-to-Me function. Also, think about what's happening in other fields that might influence your customer's behavior. When the iPod came out, it certainly changed how people used their car stereos. The winners have been those companies that adapted fast with a small change—an iPod plug-in, for example—with big consequences. The question is, can you find inspiration where no one else is looking?

Twitter @Bakedin #Small

STORIES WORTH SPREADING

Do you like to tell stories? Great innovators usually do. Leaders of great companies are seldom focused on their brand when they start their business. Instead, they focus on stories—and if those stories are powerful enough, they eventually change the world.

These stories are usually at the grassroots level. The founder is usually an inventor or user trying to change the world for himself or herself, years before anyone else sees the opportunity. In the start-up phase, these leaders inherently rely on their customers, suppliers, and employees to help develop and broaden their story. Established companies often forget this and try to distance themselves from their turbulent beginnings. But most companies would do well to revisit, and build on, their own creative history.

That's hard to do. In more developed companies,

the fluid, organic process of creating the stories necessary to fuel marketing and product design has usually been replaced by a linear process. When the product-first, marketing-second linear process becomes established in a company, each participant is judged by what he or she adds to the story and, in the process, changes it slightly to put his or her mark on it. The result, as we've discussed here, is that too often the product tells a different story from the marketing.

This is another reason why we think that rather than relying on a more linear process, companies must instead focus on open collaboration. It's the only organic way to ensure that everyone involved is contributing to the same narrative, one that inspires everything from product creation to marketing in a powerful alignment.

Tinker Hatfield is one guy who's proven to be very good at finding the right story. As Nike's creative guru, he has been responsible for many of its most innovative shoes, from Air Jordans to the 180 running shoe and the Cross-Trainer. Tinker creates magic through his ability to look at the world holistically. Yet he found himself struggling to find inspiration for the twentieth anniversary Air Jordan shoe. It was an important shoe—after all, the Air Jordan had transformed the entire Nike brand—and he needed to tell the right story with it.

His goal was to use the shoe as a canvas to look

back at Jordan's life and tell the stories Jordan had inspired. The idea of using the product itself to tell such stories—as opposed to using traditional marketing for that purpose—can be unfamiliar territory for a large company. While many entrepreneurial companies accomplish this intuitively, most bigger companies, as we've discussed, really struggle to figure this out.

In his search for inspiration, Hatfield found the central theme for the Jordan XX design in an article about Dave Monette, a sought-after trumpet maker based in Portland, who creates horns for the likes of Wynton Marsalis. In particular, Hatfield was struck by a special touch Monette builds into the trumpets he designs for Marsalis: he has a jeweler engrave symbols on the bell of the trumpet that remind Marsalis of important and inspiring moments in his career. If it works for trumpets, Hatfield realized, why can't it work for a shoe? (In this respect, Hatfield was borrowing from outside his category—a time-honored design technique, as we've seen.) After spending some time with Monette and seeing some of his trumpets, Hatfield spent four days with Jordan, listening to him relive his most important memories. All the while, he was sketching.

The result was a mid-shoe strap decorated with a mosaic of some 200 lasered graphics depicting important pieces of Jordan's life story, as told by Jordan himself. Other Nike designers who had helped design versions of the Air Jordan over the last two decades added to the graphics collection, as well. In addition, many of the shoe's other features also told Jordan stories—like the 69 dimples along the side, one for each point in Jordan's highest-scoring game. Featuring enough messages to fill a college course on the life of Michael Jordan, the XX is the sneaker equivalent of the song American Pie.

"Maybe the most important [graphic] for MJ," Hatfield told us, pointing to a spot on the shoe, "is this toolbox. It says Pops, which is what he called his dad, who was gifted with his hands and could fix anything."

By starting with not just any story, but the *right* story—in a way that aligned product design and marketing from the beginning, rather than adding them in piecemeal—Hatfield provided the inspiration for a shoe in which the marketing was completely baked into the product. The story resonated with customers, as well: it sold out in a single day.

Stories work well at connecting people because they are baked into our DNA. Our stories, and the ability to share them, are what make us human. They bring context and meaning to everything we do. Stories carry our hopes, dreams, and values. They arouse our curiosity and invite us to wonder. They resonate deeply in our souls. And, told well, they stick in our minds forever.

Whenever a company consciously and effectively tells its own stories, others begin telling them, too. The stories are told and retold in the company's hallways. They are also told at the distribution center, at the suppliers' factories, on the retail floor, in the media, and even in the homes of customers. But companies don't always recognize how their stories are being told. Worse, they don't always give the subject the honest consideration it deserves. But to be successful, proper consideration for a story is essential to your company's success—because a story is almost always the shorthand consumers are using to understand you. And if you want to add to your story or change the course of your story, it has to fit to stick.

If you're Toyota and your story is Japanese reliability, you may have to add something to your story about a plant in the U.S. if you want to sell full-size trucks to American drivers. But the story will work. If you're Honda and your story is small economical cars and you want to get into the luxury segment, you might not be able to make that story fit. So you'll need to start a new story: the Acura story.

To be successful, a brand's story must connect with a larger conversation that's happening in the culture. If it doesn't, the story seems out of sync. Marketing based on an out-of-sync story goes unnoticed and products go unsold. When we started working with Burger King a few years ago, we resurrected the story of "Have It Your Way." Originally, this was a marketing slogan. But we wanted to put it right at the heart of the

Burger King story.

We noticed that in the broader culture, choice was burgeoning everywhere. Consumers were demanding participation in everything from the products they were buying to marketing. Now, Have It Your Way is the central story told at Burger King, from marketing to product creation. It inspired the idea for Chicken Fries—premium chicken cut like french fries and served in a cup, so it was easier to eat protein on the go. It also influenced packaging. We created the fry pod, which allowed french fry cups to fit into standard cup-holders in cars. By connecting Burger King's story to a greater cultural story, the brand and its products have had unprecedented success.

The power of story can help companies face even the largest global challenges. Today, most businesses face strategic questions that are so big they can feel unmanageable, or even incomprehensible. The very size of global strategic issues can lead to the feeling that it doesn't really matter what individuals might think. The strategic questions create their own dynamic that must be overcome before solutions can be found.

Storytelling is the best tool for dealing with the immenseness of such strategic issues. These kinds of stories must provide a kind of plausibility, coherence, and rationality that enable people to make sense of the immensely complex challenges that the marketplace presents. A powerful story can hold the different

elements of a strategic question together long enough to energize and inspire people to action. Such a story can give people the ability to make sense of whatever happens in the context of their own lives, allowing them to contribute their own input toward creating the future of the company.

RECIPE

Before you can align your story with marketing and product design, you have to know it intimately. It all starts internally. Studies have shown that employees are most engaged when they understand where they're going. From the understanding comes a deeper commitment. To build its story internally, a company must answer these sorts of questions: Who are we? Where did we come from? What do we do? What do we care about? Can you answer these? If so, you're ready to start telling powerful stories with your products and marketing, and then you have the ability to change culture.

The Shakers had their founding story. It influenced everything they did. Think about powerful stories that are told inside your company. Is there a founding story? Herb Kelleher, the founder of Southwest Airlines, knows his. His vision for the airline was getting passengers to their destinations when they want to go, on time, at the lowest cost, and, most important, having fun doing it. This vision created a narrative that customers can connect with and employees can have a great time rallying behind.

People crave a human connection with the companies

whose products they buy. A cornerstone of good branding is good storytelling—but it's a two-way street. Companies must constantly evolve their *own* story by listening to and understanding their customer's stories. From here, they can create deeper, more relevant stories that evolve and continually change culture.

Twitter @Bakedin #Stories

DIFFERENCES HAVE TO LOOK DIFFERENT

Maybe you have a new idea. Maybe you have a new system. Maybe you have a new sustainable model. Whatever its story, you have to make sure to design your product so it doesn't get lost in the same old story of its broader category. Remember Eco-Products? The brilliant biodegradable process Eco-Products designed to make a better disposable fork created a wonderfully engaging story. But the actual utensil looks pretty much like any other plastic fork.

Part of baking in the marketing means that market-changing differences have to *look* different. Exhibit A: the Apple iPod. The marketing was baked into the product function: Think of the ease of use, the entirely new music ecosystem. It was different—and Apple truly overcommitted to making it look different. When the iPod was released, there were lots of MP3 players already out there, in addition to innumerable portable CD players that were still on the market. When you think about what it meant to look different in that particular sea of options, it's important to remember that many, if not most, of these devices were kept in people's pockets. No amount of design was going to communicate that something was different here if it was stuffed inside somebody's jacket.

Somebody at Apple must have thought very hard about this because it did a brilliant thing—maybe the only thing that could have worked. Apple made the earbuds and cord white. White. Not just a *different* color from black, but the *opposite* of every other cord and earbud set out there. Suddenly, there was no chance that anybody listening to an iPod could be confused with somebody listening to anything else. And that bright white cord made every single contact any of us had with anybody using an iPod into a marketing moment. And it's no mistake that the advertising capitalized on this narrative: suddenly, the culture was full of ads that simply depicted the white earbuds silhouetted against an image of a body writhing in musical joy.

Have you ever heard of Y water? There is a chance you have. The company's mission is to make organic, nutrient-rich, low-calorie drinks for kids—or anybody. In a crowded category, it has a unique story, and it didn't make the mistake of putting that story into a generic package. Nope. The Y water bottle doesn't look like any bottle you've ever seen. It looks like a cross between a three-dimensional Y and a molecule. The bottle is recyclable—or you can actually go to the FedEx office and ship them back to the company free of charge (something the company calls Y to Y).

But before you send those bottles back, you might want to play with them. That's right, play with them. The bottles can actually be joined together to make things. They're like a giant tinker toy. We suggested a bottle for 7UP years ago that would do a similar thing (about those big companies and their silos and "innovation processes"…). Y water obviously understands that innovation in the beverage category probably shouldn't end with the liquid. So now kids have another reason to ask for something better to drink. The drink becomes a toy, and when you're done, it can go back to the company. That's different. And the company made the difference *look* different. These guys are growing rapidly in a crowded category. Stay tuned.

RECIPE

What's different about what you're doing?
- A unique and more sustainable manufacturing process?
- A different set of longer-lasting materials?
- A streamlined functionality?
- Easy-to-open packaging (now, there's an innovation someone needs to develop)?

Instead of just advertising the benefits, think about making the differences visible in your product design. If you do it right, not only will your products be more distinct but your competitors will also have a harder time copying them. In fact, you might want your competitors to start copying them. Think of the iPod earbuds. The white cords are so synonymous with the iPod that whenever anyone is wearing a pair of white earbuds, we all just assume that they're carrying an iPod. Apple can just sit back, thank its competitors for helping promote its products, and start baking the next disruptive marketing idea into its next generation of products.

Twitter @Bakedin #Different

A ROSE BY ANY OTHER NAME WOULD NOT *SELL* AS SWEETLY

William Shakespeare wrote the immortal line, but it's doubtful he really believed it. Otherwise *Romeo and Juliet* would have been titled *Everybody Dies*.

The rose sits atop the list of top ten flowers by sales volume. But when you ask people to make a list of the best-smelling flowers, the rose is often bested by the lowly gardenia and frangipani. It's worth noting just how much a good name can help—and even more important, how much a bad name can hold you back. With their names, the gardenia and the frangipani can't even break into the top ten in flower sales. "My love is like a frangipani" just doesn't have the marketing baked in.

When designing anything, it's important to consider

the name as part of the design. It is not a function that should be separated from the design process. It is not something that should be strapped on at the last minute. And it is not something that should ever, ever, ever be underestimated in its marketing power. The name alone can bake in the product's marketing.

One of the all-time best product names has to be the Volkswagen Beetle. It's somewhat ironic that this name was never fully adopted by VW. In fact, it was first used in the company's U.S. advertising in 1967, but it was never used corporately until the launch of the New Beetle in 1998. But the Beetle it was, and the name said it all. The name said it was small and round and funny looking, but also tough and friendly. And the name meant it wasn't a mistake—it was supposed to look like this. It meant it was a living thing. It's interesting to note that in the U.K., where the car was known more as a Volkswagen Type One, it never experienced the cultural resonance or bond that we felt for it in America. Nope, over there they fell in love with the MINI (another great name).

A few years ago, we had an assignment that really showed us the startling power of names. Even we were surprised. Volkswagen had asked us to work on an advertising campaign for the Golf. The Golf is an amazing car, one of the best-selling in the entire world. But in the U.S., it has always floundered. We wanted to understand why. When we dug into the history, we found that sales had been steadily declining for the last 15 years from a peak of 250,000 cars a year to a current level of 30,000 cars. Almost a 90 percent slide. And when we looked back at that peak year, we found an interesting fact. The car had a different name back then. A cute name. A name that said quick and nimble and small: the Rabbit.

As we dug further, we found that dozens of Rabbit clubs existed all around the country full of devoted fans. But what shocked us was that we couldn't find a single Golf fan site or club. This couldn't be a coincidence. After more due diligence, Volkswagen of North America asked the parent company Volkswagen AG for a variance in the name. This is not a small request. Every international brand prefers to have global names, so the rationale for a variance has to be dramatic. It was. The car got its old name back and a new ad campaign to go with it. The advertising was fine, but it wasn't good enough to explain a sales increase from 30,000 the year before as a Golf to 50,000 as the Rabbit. And the advertising campaign can't explain all the clubs that sprang up, all the T-shirts that were sold, or all the tattoos people got. Nope. That is all in the name. Proving that a Rabbit by any other name does not sell as sweetly, either.

RECIPE

How do you name your products? Most companies just use the industry norm, that is, if it's about numbers, then they use numbers. This happens a lot with technology, where the focus is on the function of the product. That's okay. But just think how much more momentum products would get if they had a name that made a connection to culture. Do you remember the story about the Flip video camera? What a powerful story—and name.

In addition to numbers, companies like to use place names for their products. The U.S. car industry has gotten really good at this. Unfortunately, this doesn't work well, either. The name just doesn't fit with the product, or at worst, it says something the product isn't saying.

Think about your products. Is there a way to bake in names that mean something to the culture in which your products live?

Twitter @Bakedin #Rose

THE POWER OF PERFECTLY WRONG

When you're trying to design a product in which the marketing is baked in, it's necessary to get people talking about your new idea. One of the most powerful ways to do this is to design your product perfectly wrong. The key here is in the word "perfectly."

To design something wrong is easy (so easy that apparently everybody is doing it). A little wrong is no good, and a lot wrong is even worse—whereas perfectly wrong can be perfect. The key? The wrongness must be in direct opposition to prevailing wisdom. The world is filled with perfectly wrong successes. A shoe with the toe higher than the heel? Earth shoes. A car shaped like a box? Scion xB. A doll that instead of being designed to be cute is designed to be ugly? Uglydoll.

Uglydolls are the creation of independent toy designers David Horvath and Sun-Min Kim. The first Uglydoll appeared in 2002, and they just kept selling out. Retailers were getting harassed by buyers who wanted to know when there would be more. It may have been an accident, but these dolls had an instant advantage in the marketplace. Their marketing was baked in by the simple fact that these dolls were perfectly wrong; they were the direct opposite of what cute was supposed to be (which is one useful characterization of the opposite of what a doll is supposed to be). The Uglydolls had oddly shaped heads and very noncute features, like zombie eyes and pointy teeth. They weren't just *less* cute than other dolls; they couldn't even be described as having below-average looks. Nope, they were ugly—and in that, they were perfectly wrong. In 2006, Uglydolls were awarded the Specialty Toy of the Year award by the Toy Industry of America. Today, Uglydolls are even in Nordstrom. And here we thought Nordstrom had a policy against ugly things.

Another recent favorite of ours in the perfectly

wrong category is a new acne care product called Frutels. The Frutels website says Frutels is a "targeted formula of vitamins and minerals that delivers powerful antioxidants and micronutrients to support your body's defenses against the causes of acne." It isn't something you rub on your face; unlike most acne products, you ingest it, and it works from the inside out.

This formula could undoubtedly have been put in a drink, something refreshing and clean tasting. Or it would have been easy to make it into a chewable vitamin formulation. Either of those ideas would have been okay. Maybe each one would have a little wrong in its own right.

But the folks at Frutels chose the perfectly wrong delivery system for its acne treatment. The company chose a chocolate candy—the very thing that legend has said causes pimples—as the way to deliver its medicine. Suddenly, the mind is filled with thoughts and questions and jokes, and pretty soon the tongue is wagging, too. The chocolate idea has captured everybody's attention. There is an unstated but glaring subtext to putting acne medicine in chocolate: Either you're crazy, or you're confident that it works that well.

The good news for Frutels is it got our attention, and the attention of a lot of other people, and the product seems to be getting good marks for efficacy from a lot of people, too.

RECIPE

What happens if you did things wrong? Are any of your competitors doing it wrong, too? If not, think about how you would do things if you wanted to do them perfectly wrong. You can design your product the wrong way, like the Uglydoll, or have the wrong ingredients, like Frutels. Or you could do something even more radical. Bruce Mau helped Shaw Industries turn the carpet business upside down by focusing on a new system to implement the company's values in everything it does. The system, Shaw Green Edge, has given the company not only a different philosophy, but it has also helped identify some of the inherent flaws with the way the entire industry has been run. Similarly, Patagonia has taken the wrong position in the clothing business by calling into question many business-as-usual practices that have been done for decades.

Twitter @Bakedin #Wrong

MAKE YOUR PRODUCT TALK

Many of the massive brand successes of recent years have shocked many people with their ability to create tremendous awareness without any traditional advertising—or in some cases, seemingly without any marketing at all. The most famous of these is Google. It's doubtful that when Google started, its founders knew they were creating a media company, perhaps the largest the world has ever known. They were skeptical of using advertising as a way to monetize their service.

They didn't know that Google AdWords would become the way to monetize their service, and that pushing up advertising messages would become Google's basic business model. What they did know was that if they built the best product, people would come; and when they did come—in the hundreds of millions—Google remade itself into a media company.

Media companies have never had to advertise because the world comes to them for information.

Doing media on such a mass scale isn't something we can all reproduce—just ask Yahoo! or Ask.com. But there are lots of ways to offer media to your customers to leverage your marketing. Threadless is doing it. Flip is doing it.

Just like Google, the *New York Times* was never a company that needed to buy advertising. It was a company that *sold* advertising. It isn't news that newspaper companies are struggling these days because so many of us now get our news online. But it's less well known that a big piece of the revenues the newspaper companies have lost has been captured by another web company: Craigslist. A big, stable profit center for many of the nation's newspapers has always been classified advertising. When Craigslist did classified advertising better and cheaper, it put a lot of local papers out of business. Many of them never saw this coming.

Craigslist CEO Jim Buckmaster told the *New York Times* in 2005, "We pay zero attention to brand. We never use the word internally. We do zero advertising. We don't have a logo…. And now we're told we have the strongest brand ever for a company our size. That's pretty ironic." He's right about everything—except the irony.

Creating a media company, even a small one, is a powerful thing. Facebook has become a media company. So has YouTube. Both of these companies have something else in common—they are struggling to figure out how to monetize their service. Other companies are coming at it from the other direction. They already know how to make money, but they want the marketing bump that comes from building social media into their business models.

Best Buy has had tremendous success in this area with its internal social network, Blue Shirt Nation. And it freely admits it was a fluke. "It's a fluke because we didn't know enough at the beginning to say what it would be," Gary Koelling and Steve Bendt, the founders of Blue Shirt Nation, told us. What started as a place for a couple of advertising guys to get a better sense of what employees were thinking has become a 20,000-member community that actually makes Best Buy better. Best Buy corporate quickly saw the benefit of this community. Blue Shirt Nation has created more trust between Best Buy corporate and its stores by using the power of transparency.

And it's not just a place for employees to grumble. A recent challenge to convince the community to participate in the company 401(k) program created a 30 percent increase in enrollment. Try that any other way and see how much it costs. The Blue Shirt Nation community debates the best way to help the customer, the quality of different products, and the worthiness of services. And if you believe in transparency and its ability to create real and differentiating trust with the customer, you have to think about the next step for this fluke of a community. If it works internally, why wouldn't it work externally, too?

Our fear of losing control of the brand holds back most marketers, but as we've discussed—and as more companies learn every day—the truth of what your customers think of your brand is already out there (or soon will be) on the blogs and in coffee shops and other gathering places. Would you rather make how well your company communicates with customers a part of why people trust you, or a part of why they *don't* trust you? That is the only question left.

Right now, Blue Shirt Nation is only accessible to Best Buy employees. But who knows—by the time you read this book, that might have changed.

What would Google Search be if it didn't just deliver search media but also played in social media? It might look a little like something called StumbleUpon.

StumbleUpon has created a community of users that can view and share and follow one another and their favorite places on the Web. Privacy isn't an issue;

unlike with Google's search history, you only share your favorites; users and followers build fame and function for one another in a way similar to how Twitter works. And it is working for StumbleUpon. In a few short years, it has gained a loyal following of eight million registered users (in 2009), which means it is making its way across the techie gap into the mainstream. The sense of discovery gives users a good feeling about StumbleUpon, but it also allows them to feel good about their part in the process. Nobody ever went to the poorhouse making people feel good about themselves.

RECIPE

Think about how you talk currently. Do you use traditional advertising and PR with centralized controls? Or is there a vibrant community of communicators inside your company? Even if you might not know it, there are probably dozens, if not hundreds, of people inside your company who are blogging, tweeting, or even stumbling. Wouldn't it be cool to take all of that communication and turn it loose to make more people passionate about your company and what it does? We know—there is probably some rule in an employee handbook somewhere that spells out guidelines for what people can and can't talk about. Sure, every company has secrets that need to be kept secret; but most of these handbook guidelines may have become a bit antiquated. It's probably time to change them.

Once they're changed, it's time to start allowing

people who work with you to use the new media to your advantage. Threadless has it dialed—its internal folks are communicating in a way that has invited passionate fans who want to participate in the culture of the company. By becoming more like a media company and putting communications at the center of your company, magic starts to happen. Think about how you might bake more media into your products.

Twitter @Bakedin #Talk

THE POWER OF AN ABSOLUTE

Going to extremes with a product is a powerful marketing idea. Quick, think of a handgun. There's a pretty good chance the .44 Magnum came to mind. When Clint Eastwood uttered those words, "The most powerful handgun in the world," a brand was born. If you've ever fired one, however, you know that most powerful doesn't translate to most accurate, or most reliable, or best all around. But it does translate into sales.

The most beautiful thing about stating an absolute is that these statements don't have to be what we might consider a positive. So if most powerful works, then weakest will work, too. (Maybe not for guns, but we wouldn't rule it out.) If fastest works, then so will slowest. If heaviest works, so will lightest. If loudest works, so will quietest, and so on. What doesn't work very well is the middle: quieter, faster, lighter. If you're not quietest, fastest, lightest, which is to say if you can't figure out a way to become an absolute, then move on.

There was an electric car that was making the news in early 2009. We saw it featured on a morning news show, and the company reps kept mentioning it was the second-fastest street-legal car on the road. It was so upsetting. Even the interviewer wanted to say "fastest," but kept correcting himself. The amount of energy that company is going to have to expend to tell its "second-fastest" story is probably equal to the effort needed to put a man on the moon. And all we could keep thinking was, if you're that close, for goodness sake, figure out how to get to that absolute. Maybe set your sights on fastest 0 to 60 or 0 to 100 mph or over a quarter-mile—there are lots of ways to cut "fastest." We all would love to tell one another the fastest car is an electric car. That would be news that would spread like wildfire, and the marketing would be done. Totally baked in.

"Smallest" was the absolute that we had a chance to work with in the U.S. launch of the MINI. With the introduction of the MINI, the BMW group was preparing to bring the smallest car to America in 2002, when small-car sales had been in a dive for more than eight years. Not surprisingly, this made everybody very nervous. SUVs dominated the American roads. They were big and getting bigger, and in focus groups many people expressed concerns about being in a small car amid all that big SUV steel and aggression. In the face of all of this, it was difficult for some people to embrace the word smallest. This makes sense; how can smallest be a good thing when small is clearly not?

The easiest way to think about it is like sets and subsets. We break the world down into categories as a coping mechanism for the onslaught of information we receive every day. So we break cars down into SUVs, small SUVs, sedans, sports cars, pickup trucks, and so on.

When we hear about something new, we want to throw it into one of our preexisting mental bins and forget about it—unless there is something special about the item that allows us to help define or redefine a category. In this respect, the product is actually helping us make better sense of the world. So in the category of small cars, there was an opportunity—an opportunity, not a given—to define the category and be heralded for it. Can anyone remember the smallest car in America prior to MINI? (We can't, and we were paid to know at one point.) So that opportunity obviously passed by a lot of people after Beetle and Honda Civic owned it.

The original thinking for MINI marketing went something to the effect, "Small on the outside—big on the inside." Well, that's not embracing small. That's not an absolute. So what you get is something in the middle. And the middle is to be avoided by all marketers at all times. The middle is death. Instead of choosing the middle we grabbed a pole, stitched up a flag, and proudly began to wave the banner of the small car. Our first salvo in the fall of 2002 was a simple all-type billboard that declared, "THE SUV BACKLASH OFFICIALLY STARTS NOW." The morning we put up the billboard, the *Wall Street Journal* ran a big story about the dominance of the SUV and how it was expected to continue for another five years. Six months later, the *Atlanta Journal-Constitution* ran an article that listed three reasons for the "SUV backlash" and included the MINI campaign as one of them. They didn't even realize we had created the phrase "SUV backlash" at the same time we started the backlash. Most important, by the time the *AJC* wrote that article, the entire year's supply of MINIs were gone. All at a time when gas was just over a buck a gallon.

RECIPE

Is there anything about your product that is absolute? Do you have any products that are the fastest? The slowest? The biggest? The smallest? The loudest? The quietest? Stop and think about your products using "er"; what can you do to stake out an "est"?

What will you need to do when someone threatens your absolute? MINI had the opportunity to protect its legacy, but when the Smart Car was introduced in the U.S., it lost its "est" (smallest) and became an "er" (smaller)—and along with it a lot of power, not only in product design but also in marketing. Try to own your "est."

Twitter @Bakedin #Absolute

MAKE WHAT'S INSIDE VISIBLE ON THE OUTSIDE

Sometimes a company works hard enough at the product design process to conceive of something truly different. And yet we've all seen these products fail. Somehow, the companies that created them were unable to convince us all of their specialness. They were different, but their form was just like everything else, so we couldn't see what was different about them on the outside. The products didn't speak to us about what made them unique, and they couldn't help us speak to others about why we were using them. So their message went unheard.

The reason why this story is so common is because it is really quite difficult to do. And it's not without its risks.

Leo Fender didn't invent the electric guitar. In fact, by the time he started tinkering around in the 1940s, electric amplified guitars had been around for ten years. But what Fender did was discard the whole idea of what a guitar should be, as well as how they had always made sound. Guitars were hollow, and

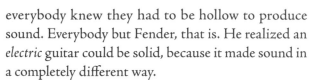

everybody knew they had to be hollow to produce sound. Everybody but Fender, that is. He realized an *electric* guitar could be solid, because it made sound in a completely different way.

In fact, this solidity was important to Fender's ultimately technological story, which was really about the control of feedback. Suddenly, now that it was solid, the electric guitar could be smaller and thinner, and it could be designed to look like something from the future. Fender didn't squander the opportunity. With the 1951 Broadcaster, which would become the legendary Telecaster, Fender created the future of sound. With the 1954 launch of the Stratocaster, he cemented in our minds what an electric guitar should look like. It was the sound of the future, and it was designed to look like the sound of the future. The Stratocaster cast off old ideas about form and function and said in a clear voice to everyone who saw it then or has seen it since, "I'm different—inside and out."

So what if your story is more subtle? One of our favorites is the story of the Nissan Xterra. Launched in the 2000 model year, the car was designed to appeal to "adventurous outdoor lifestyle consumers," or at least people who like to think of themselves that way. The advertising was good, but it would be hard to say it was fundamentally different from Ford Explorer advertising. But the Xterra had its marketing baked in. The car had visual appeal for the outdoor lifestyle consumer, with big tires, big fenders, and roof racks. But it also had one really conspicuous "hump" in the rear lift gate. That hump, it was announced, "made room for the first-aid kit."

Well, we've done lots of scary things and carried multiple first-aid kits, but we've never had to punch out a section of car body to make room for them. Nope. That hump was there to make you ask why it was there, and the answer that it was where the first-aid kit was stored was just the thing to make us all believe this vehicle really was for what Nissan was saying it was for. The hump helped get people over the hump of buying the car, and when they drove it, the hump communicated to you and everybody else just what kind of person they were. The hump made the Xterra unparalleled in magnifying the outdoorsy character of its owner. In its ninth year, it's still going strong. And so is the hump. It will be interesting to see what happens if or when the hump goes.

One of our favorite examples of turning the product inside out comes in the form of a juice box. We're not sure how popular banana juice is in Japan, but our sense is it's a bit of a new idea. If you've ever tried to juice a banana, you would know why. Banana paste: Easy. Banana juice: Not gonna happen.

When Naoto Fukasawa was asked to design the package for this novel concept, his instinct was to get out of the way and let the story out. His philosophy on design would fill a book. And it has. It's titled *Naoto Fukasawa,* and it's a must-read for anybody with even a casual interest in industrial design. His basic concept is that he believes good design is invisible. It goes away.

And it is remarkable to see what happens when this philosophy meets a banana juice box. It's worth a search online if you haven't seen it. But what happens is the box turns into a square banana. No name. No logo. No words even saying "banana juice." Just a box that looks like banana. There is no need for anything else. The juice box says juice and the banananess says banana. You have to see it to believe it. And if you do see it, and you like bananas, and you like others to see your affinity for bananas, you have to buy it.

RECIPE

Making the invisible visible is a powerful way to bake marketing into your products. Think about what's inside your products that makes them work and connects them to your customers. How can you make the power of your products visible? It could be literal, like the window Nike used to feature Air technology in the Air 180 running shoe, or how Fukasawa designed the packaging for banana juice. Or it could be subtler, like the hump on the Xterra. The key is making sure a big idea is baked into the product itself and not just the packaging. Packaging can get thrown away. Your product usually won't.

Twitter @Bakedin #Visible

DESIGN TO YOUR WEAKNESS, OR HUG THE BIG HAIRY MONSTER

Most brands and most companies have one big hairy monster. That one big issue in their relationship with consumers that keeps them up at night. It might be an aging customer base. It might be carbon emissions. It might be excessive use of natural resources. It might be labor. It might be service. It might be quality. But whatever it is, pretty much everybody has a big hairy problem with how they do business—and these days, pretty much everybody knows about it. There are no dirty little secrets anymore—just dirty stories—and there is nothing more difficult for an organization to do than to turn straight into those issues and take them head on.

Back in 2005, Wal-Mart was in a bit of a bind. While it had become the biggest retailer in the world, it was suffering from multiple PR hits that were blowing up into bigger issues. At the heart of things was Wal-Mart's perceived practice of scorched-earth global capitalism by focusing solely on lower costs without considering the environmental or human costs.

At Wal-Mart, to even bring up words like "environmental impact" must have seemed like a PR nightmare. But Wal-Mart's CEO, Lee Scott, laid out an ambitious vision of transforming the company to become more environmentally sustainable and along the way achieve two other goals: improve the company's bottom line and its reputation.

To some, it seemed a radical thought. By being more sustainable, Wal-Mart could be more profitable. But to designers familiar with sustainable systems, it actually makes perfect sense. Wal-Mart has embraced its one-time enemies and asked for input at the same time it has demanded more accountability and innovation from its suppliers. It would be easy to say, "We don't make the stuff. We just sell it." But Wal-Mart didn't. Instead, it used its clout to begin to fix its business.

Imagine the power in Wal-Mart, the world's biggest retailer, demanding more accountability from its vendors. For instance, Wal-Mart mandated that it would only sell concentrated liquid laundry detergent. By forcing its suppliers to change, Wal-Mart saved more than 400 million gallons of water, 95 million pounds of plastic resin, 125 million pounds of cardboard, and 520,000 gallons of diesel fuel over three years.

"Lee pushed me," A. G. Lafley, CEO of P&G, told the *New York Times* in 2009, and "we totally, totally changed the way we manufacture liquid laundry detergents in the U.S. and, now, around the world."

Another example is fluorescent bulbs—Wal-Mart sold 100 million of these in 2007. When Wal-Mart wanted to change from incandescent to fluorescent because they were better for the environment, suppliers like General Electric (GE) had to make a bulb that lasted longer and needed to be replaced less often, resulting in fewer sales. But when Wal-Mart suggests something, even folks like GE transform the way they do business.

While these and other examples have been good for society, they've also been good for Wal-Mart's bottom line. When Wal-Mart changed the design of its delivery trucks, the trucks were made 25 percent more fuel efficient, saving the company an estimated $500 million in fuel costs over the next 10 years.

Wal-Mart has learned that doing good does well, being one of only two stocks on the NYSE to rise in 2008. Lee Scott was quoted in the same article in the *New York Times* saying, "It wasn't a matter of telling our story better. We had to create a better story."

Wal-Mart designed a new vision beginning with its perceived biggest weakness and working out from there. This approach is in the very early stages, but it has already made a difference in some very practical ways, and it has even begun to make a difference in how people who formerly rejected all things Wal-Mart are seeing the brand. In a single brilliant flanking move, Wal-Mart has let Target be "the designer big box" and has begun to reshape itself as "the greener, more sustainable big box." If Wal-Mart follows through, it will not only capture Middle America but the coasts, too, because truly sustainable business models will ultimately capture the high ground in all categories. For the sake of the planet, we all have to hope it stays with the plan. But it might be time to begin to get your head around the idea of Wal-Mart being cooler than Target.

Video game makers have been living with a big hairy monster for quite some time now. America's children have become less and less active over the years, and the video game industry has become a convenient target for parents who don't know how to get their kids outside, and politicians who have cut the budget of school physical fitness programs. To most video game makers, it probably seemed like the only option that would make their detractors happy would be to go out of business. But one company listened to the detractors and gave the big hairy monster a big hug. Nintendo was reading all the same bad press as everybody else, but somehow it saw an opportunity, an opportunity that probably just looked like more bad news for Nintendo, which had seen its hardware sales shrink to half of what they had been two decades ago.

In 2006, more powerful systems from Microsoft and Sony dominated the market, and the only thing that seemed to matter was processing power for better graphics. Nintendo couldn't win at this game, so it changed the rules—it built Wii, a more affordable, motion-controlled machine with simple graphics that blew up the market and made gamers out of everyone from young girls to grandma and grandpa.

Early on, a decision was made that Wii would use a cheaper chip, making high-end graphics impossible. It was the motion-control feature that would give consumers a whole new way to interact with games, a way that created some very sticky imagery. Game players were moving, and moving fast and furiously. It was all over the news because it was exactly the opposite of what we expected from a computer game console. And it made for great TV. Games were supposed to make people into couch potatoes, not Richard Simmons. Knowing that how people first reacted with the console would be the key to word of mouth and sales, Nintendo boldly decided to sell the console with the killer app Wii Sports included for just $250. Suddenly, gamers everywhere were swinging at balls and boxing and bowling. In many cases, the Wii didn't replace the Sony Microsoft console but instead wound up sitting alongside it—proof that Nintendo had created a whole new category of gaming.

RECIPE

What's the big hairy monster in your category? Is it an aging population? For a long time, Cadillac was faced with the fact that most of its customers were dying. Is it a new technology? Is it, like Wal-Mart, the environment? Or, like Nintendo, the effects its industry was having on customers? Face it. Every business has big hairy monsters.

Think about how you can embrace the big hairy monster. What can you do to start a dialogue about your monster? Can you engage your customers? Can it be reflected in your product design and your communications? Just like Wal-Mart, you'll probably not be able to tame the monster, or even necessarily solve the problem, but you can start working on it. The key is to start a movement with momentum. Customers love it when they see consistent behavior in the right direction, and they want to support companies that face up to their big hairy monsters.

Twitter @Bakedin #Monster

PART THREE:

THE WAY FORWARD

A s often happens in the midst of writing a book, the world has changed. This time— over the past two years or so—it seems the world has changed a lot. Many things that we have taken for granted in business, like constant growth and easy credit, have come to an end.

While some might think this is a small speed bump in our economic history, we think something larger is going on here. We think this might be the start of a deep reconfiguration of society, brought on by a combination of widely varied factors ranging from environmental degradation to new medical issues caused by the diminishing effectiveness of antibiotics to the deep greed and narcissism caused by unregulated financial engineering. And last, there has been the lack of leadership and the profound mismanagement from our political system. We are now in a situation where it's difficult to find anyone or anything to blame. There seems to be a problem with our entire cultural and political model.

Some might look at this with regret and fear. And we have had our regrets and fears, as well. But we watched them sail by. And we now view today as a time of great opportunity and hope. Finding a new way will be difficult. A new, more holistic view of the world needs to emerge, but it must start with optimism if it is to succeed. At the 2005 TED conference at Oxford, Craig Venter said he wasn't sure whether the optimists or the pessimists were right, but he knew this: it was the optimists who were going to get something done.

A new way of doing business fueled by this optimism seems to be emerging. Such optimism comes from feeling in control and from the knowledge that you're making a positive impact on society. Companies that are leading this paradigm shift bake social and environmental responsibility into both their products and their marketing. They haven't found the whole answer, but they're finding pieces of it. Companies like Whole Foods, Patagonia, and Interweave Carpets have been doing it for years, and they're considered some of today's strongest brands, mixing marketing and product design deep within their culture. Their ability to abolish internal silos and use their business to pursue a greater social good in everything they do has helped each of them draw a great following. Their customers become more than just brand advocates— they're advocates for those companies' philosophies and practitioners of those philosophies in their own lives and their own businesses.

When we began this book, we saw design and innovation as great ways to gain a competitive business advantage. But in the ensuing months, we've come to realize that design and innovation are keys to the survival of this planet. Rapid innovation in the design of our transportation systems, our power systems, our healthcare systems, our social systems, and even our economic systems is our only path to sustainability. The principles of effective innovation will have to be embraced by most of humanity for us to solve the problems we now face. In this respect, we'll have to change. This may seem daunting, but isn't change what humankind is really all about? We suspect more and more that static ideas and the static institutions are an illusion—and the illusionists are losing their ability to distract us anymore.

Perhaps the idea of "brand" itself is a distraction we no longer need or want. The idea that people can use a brand to tell others a little bit about themselves can't survive in a world where people already understand their innate selves. The idea of a brand being used to help create a personal identity can't survive in a world where identity is a given.

As consciousness increases, we don't need brands. We need something more real.

In a number of the examples we've come across in researching this book, it became evident that another theme was coming through. The greatest examples of products that marketed themselves demonstrated that they had moved *beyond* being brands. Maybe a brand was the best most companies could hope for, but with advances in technology, the best companies and products are creating systems that answer entire aspects of our lives. Systems don't ask you to know their story because you are already a part of their story. Systems don't ask to be a part of your identity because they are already a part of how you live your life. And systems don't hope for brand loyalty because they shape themselves to how you use them. You aren't loyal to a brand. You're loyal to what you've created. This is the power of systems. And although many of the best examples seem to be coming out of the digital space, the reality is that they are less about where and more about everywhere. A great system can be accessed wherever and whenever the customer needs it.

While creating a system is a worthy goal, change starts with small steps. By mixing marketing and product design, you're taking a powerful first step. We hope we've helped you realize that creativity is the ultimate business weapon by taking a systematic approach to combining the two.

This is only the beginning. We hope you'll look at these 28 rules for baking your marketing into your products as a starting point, not a definitive list. You're sure to discover more of your own rules. We hope you'll be willing to share them with us and the rest of the *Baked In* community @bakedin on Twitter or on our blog, www.bakedin.com. By using the power of collaboration, *Baked In* can become more than a static book—it can be the start of a conversation and a source of inspiration to find new ways to connect more deeply to your community of customers and fans, and lay the foundation to a system of your own.

ABOUT THE AUTHORS

Alex Bogusky joined Crispin and Porter Advertising in 1989 as an art director. He became the creative director five years later, a partner in 1997, and a co-chairman in January 2008. Under Alex's direction, Crispin Porter + Bogusky grew to more than 900 employees, with offices in Miami, Boulder, Los Angeles, London, and Sweden. Alex's work has won hundreds of top industry awards. He was inducted into the American Advertising Federation's Hall of Achievement in 2002 and the Art Directors Club Hall of Fame in 2008. In 2010, he left the advertising industry and founded the FearLess Cottage.

John Winsor is founder and CEO of Victors & Spoils, the first ad agency built on crowdsourcing principles. He was formerly the vice president/executive director of strategy and innovation at Crispin Porter + Bogusky. He joined the firm in 2007, with the purchase of his research and strategy company, Radar Communications. Prior to founding Radar, Winsor built a magazine publishing company devoted to sports such as mountain biking, in-line skating, extreme skiing, and women's sports. He sold the business to Condé Nast in 1997. Winsor is also the author of *Spark: Be More Innovative Through Co-Creation*, and *Flipped: How Bottom-Up Co-Creation is Replacing Top-Down Innovation*, published by Agate B2 in paperback in 2010.